Rolling Stone

SHEET MUSIC CLASSICS VOLUME 2 · 1970s–1990s

60 SELECTIONS FROM THE

500 GREATEST SONGS OF ALL TIME

Alfred Publishing Co., Inc.
16320 Roscoe Blvd., Suite 100
P.O. Box 10003
Van Nuys, CA 91410-0003
alfred.com

ISBN-10: 0-7390-5240-3
ISBN-13: 978-0-7390-5240-2

SHEET MUSIC CLASSICS VOLUME 2 · 1970s–1990s

Rolling Stone® 500 Greatest Songs of All Time

Welcome to the ultimate jukebox: the *Rolling Stone* 500, a celebration of the greatest rock & roll songs of all time, chosen by a five-star jury of singers, musicians, producers, industry figures, critics and, of course, songwriters. The editors of *Rolling Stone* called on rock stars and leading authorities to list their fifty favorite songs, in order of preference. The 172 voters, who included Brian Wilson, Joni Mitchell and Wilco's Jeff Tweedy, were asked to select songs from the rock & roll era. They nominated 2,103 songs in virtually every pop-music genre of the past half-century and beyond, from Hank Williams to OutKast. The results were tabulated according to a weighted point system.

For this *RS* 500, the word *song* refers to both a composition and its definitive recorded performance, as a single or an album track. Bob Dylan, the Beatles and the Rolling Stones accounted for a combined total of 117 nominated songs, a measure of their unbroken reign as rock's most influential, beloved artists. Nirvana and the Clash crashed the top twenty, rubbing guitars with Chuck Berry and Jimi Hendrix.

This *RS* 500 is also a tribute to the eternal power of popular music, and great songwriting in particular, to reflect and transform the times in which we hear it. The *RS* 500 salutes the songs that move us—and the artists who create them. It is also proof that whenever you want to know what's going on, listen to the music.

ARTIST INDEX

Abba
Dancing Queen 104

Bee Gees
How Deep Is Your Love 161
Stayin' Alive 344

Black Sabbath
Iron Man 198
Paranoid 279

Bob Marley and the Wailers
No Woman, No Cry 267
Redemption Song 308

Jackson Browne
Running On Empty 312

Jeff Buckley
Hallelujah 126

Jimmy Cliff
The Harder They Come 134

Derek and the Dominos
Layla 225

Bob Dylan
Knocking on Heaven's Door 222

Eagles
Desperado 110
Hotel California 164

The Five Stairsteps
O-o-h Child 274

Roberta Flack
Killing Me Softly With His Song 216

Marvin Gaye
What's Going On 368

Grandmaster Flash and the Furious Five
The Message 256

Guns n' Roses
Sweet Child O' Mine 350

Don Henley
The Boys of Summer 94

The Jackson 5
I Want You Back 180

Michael Jackson
Beat It 24
Billie Jean 36

The Kinks
Lola 240

Led Zeppelin
Black Dog 50
Heartbreaker 143
Kashmir 204
Ramble On 300
Stairway to Heaven 334

Madonna
Like a Prayer 232

Joni Mitchell
Help Me 150

Van Morrison
Into the Mystic 192
Moondance 262

New Order
Bizarre Love Triangle 29

New York Dolls
Personality Crisis 291

Randy Newman
Sail Away 320

Parliament
Flash Light 116

Tom Petty
Free Fallin' 122

Pink Floyd
Another Brick in the Wall Part 2 20
Comfortably Numb 99
Wish You Were Here 378

Queen
Bohemian Rhapsody 60

R.E.M.
Losing My Religion 246

Radiohead
Fake Plastic Trees 138
Paranoid Android 284

Ramones
Blitzkrieg Bop 56
I Wanna Be Sedated 176

Lou Reed
Walk on the Wild Side 364

The Rolling Stones
Wild Horses 373

Simon and Garfunkel
Bridge Over Troubled Water 86

Sly and the Family Stone
Hot Fun in the Summertime 156
Thank You (Falettinme Be Mice Elf Agin) 358

The Smiths
How Soon Is Now? 172

Bruce Springsteen
Born in the U.S.A. 72
Born to Run 76
Thunder Road 325

The Staple Singers
I'll Take You There 186

Rod Stewart
Maggie May 252

Sugarhill Gang
Rapper's Delight 305

The Verve
Bitter Sweet Symphony 44

CONTENTS

TITLE	ARTIST	PAGE
Another Brick in the Wall Part 2	Pink Floyd	20
Beat It	Michael Jackson	24
Billie Jean	Michael Jackson	36
Bitter Sweet Symphony	The Verve	44
Bizarre Love Triangle	New Order	29
Black Dog	Led Zeppelin	50
Blitzkrieg Bop	Ramones	56
Bohemian Rhapsody	Queen	60
Born in the U.S.A.	Bruce Springsteen	72
Born to Run	Bruce Springsteen	76
The Boys of Summer	Don Henley	94
Bridge Over Troubled Water	Simon and Garfunkel	86
Comfortably Numb	Pink Floyd	99
Dancing Queen	Abba	104
Desperado	Eagles	110
Fake Plastic Trees	Radiohead	138
Flash Light	Parliament	116
Free Fallin'	Tom Petty	122
Hallelujah	Jeff Buckley	126
The Harder They Come	Jimmy Cliff	134
Heartbreaker	Led Zeppelin	143
Help Me	Joni Mitchell	150
Hot Fun in the Summertime	Sly and the Family Stone	156
Hotel California	Eagles	164
How Deep Is Your Love	Bee Gees	161
How Soon Is Now?	The Smiths	172
I Wanna Be Sedated	Ramones	176
I Want You Back	The Jackson 5	180
I'll Take You There	The Staple Singers	186
Into the Mystic	Van Morrison	192

CONTENTS

TITLE	ARTIST	PAGE
Iron Man	Black Sabbath	198
Kashmir	Led Zeppelin	204
Killing Me Softly With His Song	Roberta Flack	216
Knocking on Heaven's Door	Bob Dylan	222
Layla	Derek and the Dominos	225
Like a Prayer	Madonna	232
Lola	The Kinks	240
Losing My Religion	R.E.M.	246
Maggie May	Rod Stewart	252
The Message	Grandmaster Flash and the Furious Five	256
Moondance	Van Morrison	262
No Woman, No Cry	Bob Marley and the Wailers	267
O-o-h Child	The Five Stairsteps	274
Paranoid	Black Sabbath	279
Paranoid Android	Radiohead	284
Personality Crisis	New York Dolls	291
Ramble On	Led Zeppelin	300
Rapper's Delight	Sugarhill Gang	305
Redemption Song	Bob Marley and the Wailers	308
Running On Empty	Jackson Browne	312
Sail Away	Randy Newman	320
Stairway to Heaven	Led Zeppelin	334
Stayin' Alive	Bee Gees	344
Sweet Child O' Mine	Guns n' Roses	350
Thank You (Falettinme Be Mice Elf Agin)	Sly and the Family Stone	358
Thunder Road	Bruce Springsteen	325
Walk on the Wild Side	Lou Reed	364
What's Going On	Marvin Gaye	368
Wild Horses	The Rolling Stones	373
Wish You Were Here	Pink Floyd	378

Another Brick in the Wall Part 2
Pink Floyd

Written by: Roger Waters
Produced by: Bob Ezrin, Waters, David Gilmour
Released: Nov. '79 on Columbia
Charts: 25 weeks; top spot no. 1
≫**No. 375** *from Rolling Stone® Magazine's 500 Greatest Songs of All Time*

Waters' vicious attack on teachers who practice "dark sarcasm in the classroom" was inspired by the cruelty of his own schoolmasters. "The school I was at – they were really like that," Waters said. "They were so fucked up, [all] they had to offer was their own bitterness and cynicism." "Another Brick" is rendered in three versions on *The Wall*, but "Part 2" was the hit.

Appears on: The Wall (Capitol)
(Music appears on page 20)

Beat It
Michael Jackson

Written by: Jackson
Produced by: Quincy Jones
Released: Dec. '82 on Epic
Charts: 25 weeks; top spot no. 1
≫**No. 337** *from Rolling Stone® Magazine's 500 Greatest Songs of All Time*

"I wanted to write the type of rock song that I would go out and buy," said Jackson, "but also something totally different from the rock music I was hearing on Top Forty radio." The result was a throbbing dance single with a watch-my-fingers-fly guitar solo provided by Eddie Van Halen.

Appears on: Thriller (Epic)
(Music appears on page 24)

Billie Jean
Michael Jackson

Written by: Jackson
Produced by: Jackson, Quincy Jones
Released: Jan. '83 on Epic
Charts: 7 weeks; top spot no. 1

≫**No. 58** *from Rolling Stone® Magazine's 500 Greatest Songs of All Time*

Sinuous, paranoid and omnipresent: the single that made Jackson the biggest star since Elvis was a denial of a paternity suit, and it spent seven weeks at Number One. Jackson came up with the irresistible rhythm track on his home drum machine and nailed the vocals in one take. "I knew it was going to be big while I was writing it," he said. "I was really absorbed in writing it." How absorbed? He was thinking about the song while riding in his Rolls down the Ventura Freeway in California – and didn't notice the car was on fire.

Appears on: Thriller (Sony)
(Music appears on page 36)

Bitter Sweet Symphony
The Verve

Written by: Mick Jagger, Keith Richards, Richard Ashcroft
Produced by: The Verve, Christopher Marc Potter, Youth
Released: Sept. '97 on Virgin
Charts: 20 weeks; top spot no. 12
≫**No. 382** *from Rolling Stone® Magazine's 500 Greatest Songs of All Time*

Bittersweet, indeed. Since it used a sample from an orchestral version of a Rolling Stones song, the Verve hit was credited to Jagger-Richards. Ashcroft claimed it was the best song the Stones had written in twenty years.

Appears on: Urban Hymns (Virgin)
(Music appears on page 44)

Bizarre Love Triangle
New Order

Written by: Bernard Albrecht, Gillian Gilbert, Peter Hook, Stephen Morris
Produced by: New Order
Released: Oct. '86 on Qwest
Charts: 2 weeks; top spot no. 98
≫**No. 201** *from Rolling Stone® Magazine's 500 Greatest Songs of All Time*

After the death of Joy Division's Ian Curtis, his bandmates became New Order. "There's life and there's death," drummer Morris said in 1983. "We were still alive, so we thought we'd carry on doing it." New Order wrote their moody synth-pop hits in a Manchester rehearsal room next to a cemetery. Said Morris, "Fate writes the lyrics, and we do the rest."

Appears on: Substance *(Qwest)*

(Music appears on page 29)

Black Dog
Led Zeppelin

Written by: Jimmy Page, Robert Plant, John Paul Jones
Produced by: Page
Released: Nov. '71 on Atlantic
Charts: 12 weeks; top spot no. 15
»No. 294 *from Rolling Stone® Magazine's 500 Greatest Songs of All Time*

A dog meandering the grounds outside Zeppelin's studio in rural England inspired the title, but the subject was honey-dripping sex. "Things like 'Black Dog' are blatant let's-do-it-in-the-bath-type things," Plant said, "but they make their point."

Appears on: Led Zeppelin IV *(Atlantic)*

(Music appears on page 50)

Blitzkrieg Bop
Ramones

Written by: Ramones
Produced by: Craig Leon
Released: May '76 on Sire
Charts: did not chart
»No. 92 *from Rolling Stone® Magazine's 500 Greatest Songs of All Time*

In less than three minutes, this song threw down the blueprint for punk rock. It's all here on the opening track of the Ramones' debut: the buzz-saw chords, which Johnny played on his fifty-dollar Mosrite guitar; the snotty words, courtesy of drummer Tommy (with bassist Dee Dee adding the brilliant line "Shoot 'em in the back now"); and the hairball-in-the-throat vocals, sung by Joey in a faux-British accent. Recorded on the cheap at New York's Radio City Music Hall, of all places, "Blitzkrieg Bop" never made the charts; instead, it almost single-handedly created a world beyond the charts.

Appears on: Ramones *(Rhino)*

(Music appears on page 56)

Bohemian Rhapsody
Queen

Written by: Freddie Mercury
Produced by: Roy Thomas Baker
Released: Nov. '75 on Elektra
Charts: 24 weeks; top spot no. 9
»No. 163 *from Rolling Stone® Magazine's 500 Greatest Songs of All Time*

According to Queen guitarist Brian May, everyone in the band was bewildered when Mercury brought them a draft of this four-part suite – even before he told them, "That's where the operatic bits come in!" Recording technology was so taxed by the song's multitracked scaramouches and fandangos that some tapes became virtually transparent from being overdubbed so many times.

Appears on: A Night at the Opera *(Hollywood)*

(Music appears on page 60)

Born in the U.S.A.
Bruce Springsteen

Written by: Springsteen
Produced by: Springsteen, Jon Landau, Chuck Plotkin, Steve Van Zandt
Released: June '84 on Columbia
Charts: 17 weeks; top spot no. 9
»No. 275 *from Rolling Stone® Magazine's 500 Greatest Songs of All Time*

Before it became the centerpiece of Springsteen's biggest album, "U.S.A." was an acoustic protest song meant for *Nebraska*. But when Springsteen revived it with the E Street Band, Roy Bittan came up with a monster synth riff and Max Weinberg hammered out a beat like he was using M-80s for drumsticks. "We played it two times, and our second take is the record," Springsteen said. "That thing in the end with all the drums, that just kinda happened."

Appears on: Born in the U.S.A. *(Columbia)*

(Music appears on page 72)

Born to Run
Bruce Springsteen

Written by: Springsteen
Produced by: Springsteen, Mike Appel
Released: Aug. '75 on Columbia
Charts: 11 weeks; top spot no. 23
»No. 21 *from Rolling Stone® Magazine's 500 Greatest Songs of All Time*

This song's four and a half minutes took three and a half months to cut. Aiming for the impact of Phil Spector's Wall of Sound, Springsteen included strings, glockenspiel, multiple keyboards – and more than a dozen guitar tracks. The words poured out just as relentlessly, telling a story of young lovers on the highways of New Jersey. "I don't know how important the settings are in the first place," Springsteen told *Rolling Stone*. "It's the idea behind the settings. It could be New Jersey, it could be California, it could be Alaska."

Appears on: Born to Run (Columbia)
(Music appears on page 76)

The Boys of Summer
Don Henley

Written by: Henley, Mike Campbell
Produced by: Henley, Campbell, Danny Kortchmar, Greg Ladanyi
Released: Nov. '84 on Geffen
Charts: 22 weeks; top spot no. 5
»No. 416 *from Rolling Stone® Magazine's 500 Greatest Songs of All Time*

Henley gave California rock a stylish Eighties makeover with this poignant lament for his generation, featuring the famous line "Out on the road today/I saw a Deadhead sticker on a Cadillac." When the Ataris did their hit punk-rock cover version in 2003, they changed it to a Black Flag sticker – but the sentiment was the same.

Appears on: Building the Perfect Beast (Geffen)
(Music appears on page 94)

Bridge Over Troubled Water
Simon and Garfunkel

Written by: Paul Simon
Produced by: Art Garfunkel, Roy Halee, Simon
Released: Feb. '70 on Columbia
Charts: 14 weeks; top spot no. 1
»No. 47 *from Rolling Stone® Magazine's 500 Greatest Songs of All Time*

By the time Simon wrote this tribute to friendship in 1970, his partnership with Garfunkel had become strained; they even disagreed over whether Garfunkel should sing it. "He felt I should have done it," Simon said in 1972. "And many times I think I'm sorry I didn't do it." The third verse was Garfunkel's idea; Simon wrote it but has never liked it.

Appears on: Bridge Over Troubled Water (Columbia/Legacy)
(Music appears on page 86)

Comfortably Numb
Pink Floyd

Written by: David Gilmour, Roger Waters
Produced by: Bob Ezrin
Released: Dec. '79 on Columbia
Charts: did not chart
»No. 314 *from Rolling Stone® Magazine's 500 Greatest Songs of All Time*

Waters based one of the saddest drug songs ever written on a sleazy Philadelphia doctor who injected him with tranquilizers before a gig when he was suffering from hepatitis. "That was the longest two hours of my life," Waters said. "Trying to do a show when you can hardly lift your arm."

Appears on: The Wall (Capitol)
(Music appears on page 99)

Dancing Queen
Abba

Written by: Benny Andersson, Bjorn Ulvaeus, Stig Anderson
Produced by: Andersson, Ulvaeus
Released: Nov. '76 on Atlantic
Charts: 22 weeks; top spot no. 1
»No. 171 *from Rolling Stone® Magazine's 500 Greatest Songs of All Time*

Sweden's biggest musical export debuted this

song in 1976 at a ball for King Carl Gustaf on the eve of his wedding. Classic Abba, "Queen" was a disco-flavored dessert of sublime melody and pop-operatic harmonies that became the group's only U.S. Number One.

Appears on: Arrival *(Polydor)*

(Music appears on page 104)

Desperado
Eagles

Written by: Glenn Frey, Don Henley
Produced by: Bill Szymczyk
Released: April '73 on Asylum
Charts: non-single
≫**No. 494** *from Rolling Stone® Magazine's 500 Greatest Songs of All Time*

"Desperado" was the title track of the Eagles' second LP, a concept album about outlaws in the Old West. "In retrospect, I admit the whole cowboy-outlaw-rocker myth was a bit bogus," Henley said in 1987. "I don't think we really believed it; we were just trying to make an analogy."

Appears on: Desperado *(Elektra)*

(Music appears on page 110)

Fake Plastic Trees
Radiohead

Written by: Radiohead
Produced by: John Leckie
Released: March '95 on Capitol
Charts: 4 weeks; top spot no. 65
≫**No. 376** *from Rolling Stone® Magazine's 500 Greatest Songs of All Time*

Radiohead frontman Thom Yorke would describe "Fake Plastic Trees" as the song on which he found his lyrical voice. He cut the vocal, accompanying himself on acoustic guitar, in one take, then the band filled in its parts around him. Yorke said the song began as "a very nice melody which I had no idea what to do with, then you wake up and find your head singing some words to it."

Appears on: The Bends *(Capitol)*

(Music appears on page 138)

Flash Light
Parliament

Written by: George Clinton, Bernie Worrell, Bootsy Collins
Produced by: Clinton
Released: Dec. '77 on Casablanca
Charts: 16 weeks; top spot no. 16
≫**No. 199** *from Rolling Stone® Magazine's 500 Greatest Songs of All Time*

"Flash Light" is the P-Funk Nation's manifesto, spreading the gospel of funk. "We're going to get the message out," Clinton declared in 1978. "We want to put the show on Broadway – tell the story straightforward so people understand that funk mean *funk*." Keyboardist Worrell provided the bass line, after figuring out how to stack bass tones on his Moog synthesizer.

Appears on: Funkentelechy vs. the Placebo Syndrome *(Mercury)*

(Music appears on page 116)

Free Fallin'
Tom Petty

Written by: Petty, Jeff Lynne
Produced by: Lynne
Released: June '89 on MCA
Charts: 21 weeks; top spot no. 7
≫**No. 177** *from Rolling Stone® Magazine's 500 Greatest Songs of All Time*

Petty and Lynne wrote and recorded "Free Fallin'" in just two days, the first song completed for Petty's solo LP *Full Moon Fever*. "We had a multitude of acoustic guitars," Petty said of the single's Byrds-y feel. "So it made this incredibly dreamy sound." The label initially rejected the album because of a lack of hits. "So I waited six months and brought the same record back," Petty said. "And they loved it."

Appears on: Full Moon Fever *(MCA)*

(Music appears on page 122)

Hallelujah
Jeff Buckley

Written by: Leonard Cohen
Produced by: Andy Wallace
Released: Aug. '94 on Columbia
Charts: non-single
»**No. 259** *from Rolling Stone® Magazine's 500 Greatest Songs of All Time*

During his famed early gigs at the New York club Sin-é, Buckley used to break hearts with his version of this Cohen prayer. Buckley called it an homage to "the hallelujah of the orgasm" and had misgivings about his sensuous rendition: "I hope Leonard doesn't hear it." On his posthumous live album *Mystery White Boy*, Buckley turns "Hallelujah" into a medley with the Smiths' "I Know It's Over."

Appears on: Grace (Columbia)
(Music appears on page 126)

The Harder They Come
Jimmy Cliff

Written by: Cliff
Produced by: Cliff
Released: March '75 on Mango
Charts: did not chart
»**No. 341** *from Rolling Stone® Magazine's 500 Greatest Songs of All Time*

Before this song, Cliff had already won acclaim: Bob Dylan lauded his 1969 single "Vietnam" as "the best protest song ever written." But Cliff became an international star with this gospel tale of eternal rebellion, from the movie of the same name.

Appears on: The Harder They Come (Island)
(Music appears on page 134)

Heartbreaker
Led Zeppelin

Written by: Jimmy Page, Robert Plant, John Bonham, John Paul Jones
Produced by: Page
Released: Oct '69 on Atlantic
Charts: non-single
»**No. 320** *from Rolling Stone® Magazine's 500 Greatest Songs of All Time*

"Heartbreaker," like much of *Led Zeppelin II*, was recorded hit-and-run style on Zep's 1969 American tour. The awesome swagger captures the debauched mood of the band's wild early days in L.A. "Nineteen years old and never been kissed," Plant recalled in 1975. "I remember it well. It's been a long time. Nowadays we're more into staying in our room and reading Nietzsche."

Appears on: Led Zeppelin II (Atlantic)
(Music appears on page 143)

Help Me
Joni Mitchell

Written by: Mitchell
Produced by: Mitchell
Released: Feb. '74 on Asylum
Charts: 19 weeks; top spot no. 7
»**No. 282** *from Rolling Stone® Magazine's 500 Greatest Songs of All Time*

"I had attempted to play my music with rock & roll players," Mitchell said in 1979. "They'd laugh, 'Aww, isn't that cute? She's trying to tell us how to play.'" It took a jazz group – Tom Scott's L.A. Express – to realize her biggest hit, a swooning confession of love trouble.

Appears on: Court and Spark (Elektra)
(Music appears on page 150)

Hot Fun in the Summertime
Sly and the Family Stone

Written by: Sylvester Stewart (Sly Stone)
Produced by: Stone
Released: Aug. '69 on Epic
Charts: 16 weeks; top spot no. 2
»**No. 247** *from Rolling Stone® Magazine's 500 Greatest Songs of All Time*

Summer was already under way when Stone handed in this heavenly soul ballad to his label. It came out just before the Family Stone gave their legendary performance at the '69 Woodstock – as the first band to sign up for the historic festival.

Appears on: Greatest Hits (Epic)
(Music appears on page 156)

Hotel California
Eagles

Written by: Don Felder, Glenn Frey, Don Henley
Produced by: Bill Szymczyk
Released: Dec. '76 on Asylum
Charts: 19 weeks; top spot no. 1
»**No. 49** *from Rolling Stone® Magazine's 500 Greatest Songs of All Time*

"Hotel California" was rumored to be about heroin addiction or Satan worship, but Henley had more prosaic things on his mind: "We were all middle-class kids from the Midwest," he said. "'Hotel California' was our interpretation of the high life in Los Angeles." (That doesn't preclude heroin or Satan.) A problem arose when the band, recording in Miami, was unable to re-create Felder's twelve-string intro and twin-guitar coda. Panicked, Felder called his housekeeper in L.A. and sent her digging through tapes in his home studio so she could play his demo back over the phone.

Appears on: Hotel California (Elektra)

(Music appears on page 164)

How Deep Is Your Love
Bee Gees

Written by: Barry Gibb, Maurice Gibb, Robin Gibb
Produced by: Barry Gibb, Maurice Gibb, Robin Gibb, Karl Richardson, Albhy Galuten
Released: Sept. '77 on RSO
Charts: 33 weeks; top spot no. 1
»**No. 366** *from Rolling Stone® Magazine's 500 Greatest Songs of All Time*

The first single from the *Saturday Night Fever* soundtrack was not a disco track but this slow jam. The Bee Gees' work for the film was recorded during a famed two-and-a-half-week-long session at a château in northern France, where, according to Barry Gibb, "six classic lesbian porno scenes [were] filmed."

Appears on: Saturday Night Fever (Polygram)

(Music appears on page 161)

How Soon Is Now?
The Smiths

Written by: Johnny Marr, Morrissey
Produced by: John Porter
Released: Feb. '85 on Sire
Charts: did not chart
»**No. 486** *from Rolling Stone® Magazine's 500 Greatest Songs of All Time*

Morrissey cribbed the line "The heir to nothing in particular" from George Eliot's *Middlemarch*. But guitarist Marr had another reference in mind: Derek and the Dominos. "I wanted an intro that was almost as potent as 'Layla,'" he said. "When [it] plays in a club or a pub, everyone knows what it is." Mission accomplished.

Appears on: Meat Is Murder (Warner Bros.)

(Music appears on page 172)

I Wanna Be Sedated
Ramones

Written by: Ramones
Produced by: Tommy Erdelyi, Ed Stasium
Released: Oct. '78 on Sire
Charts: did not chart
»**No. 144** *from Rolling Stone® Magazine's 500 Greatest Songs of All Time*

The greatest god-does-the-road-ever-suck song, "I Wanna Be Sedated" was written by Joey Ramone, who at the time was suffering from severe teakettle burns and had to fly to London for a gig. Plagued by obsessive-compulsive disorder and various other ailments, Joey always had a rough time touring. "Put me in a wheelchair/And get me to the show/Hurry hurry hurry/Before I go loco!" he rants. The sound is equally pissed-off: Johnny's guitar solo – the same note, sixty-five times in a row – is the ultimate expression of his anti-artifice philosophy; the bubblegum-pop key change that follows it, though, is pure Joey.

Appears on: Road to Ruin (Rhino)

(Music appears on page 176)

I Want You Back
The Jackson 5

Written by: Freddie Perren, Fonce Mizell, Deke Richards, Berry Gordy Jr.
Produced by: Perren, Mizell, Richards, Gordy
Released: Nov. '69 on Motown
Charts: 19 weeks; top spot no. 1
》**No. 120** *from Rolling Stone® Magazine's 500 Greatest Songs of All Time*

"I Want You Back" was the song that introduced Motown to the futuristic funk beat of Sly Stone and James Brown. It also introduced the world to an eleven-year-old Indiana kid named Michael Jackson. The five dancing Jackson brothers became stars overnight, as Michael yelped his lead vocals with boyish fervor. "I Want You Back" remains one of hip-hop's favorite beats, sampled everywhere from Kris Kross' "Jump" to Jay-Z's "Izzo (H.O.V.A.)."

***Appears on: The Ultimate Collection** (Motown)*

(Music appears on page 180)

I'll Take You There
The Staple Singers

Written by: Alvertis Isbell
Produced by: Al Bell
Released: June '72 on Stax
Charts: 15 weeks; top spot no. 1
》**No. 276** *from Rolling Stone® Magazine's 500 Greatest Songs of All Time*

It was a good day's work at Stax in 1971 when the Staples cut both "Respect Yourself" and "I'll Take You There." The latter – a funk vamp promising heavenly or sexual devotion, depending on your perspective – was "written on the spot," said bassist David Hood.

***Appears on: Bealtitude: Respect Yourself** (Stax)*

(Music appears on page 186)

Into the Mystic
Van Morrison

Written by: Morrison
Produced by: Morrison
Released: March '70 on Warner Bros.
Charts: non-single
》**No. 480** *from Rolling Stone® Magazine's 500 Greatest Songs of All Time*

"Into the Mystic" is one of Morrison's warmest ballads, an Otis Redding-style reverie with acoustic guitar and horns. The lyrics are truly mysterious: "People say, 'What does this mean?'" said Morrison. "A lot of times I have no idea what I mean. That's what I like about rock & roll – the concept. Like Little Richard – what does he mean? You can't take him apart; that's rock & roll to me."

***Appears on: Moondance** (Warner Bros.)*

(Music appears on page 192)

Iron Man
Black Sabbath

Written by: Black Sabbath
Produced by: Rodger Bain
Released: Feb. '71 on Warner
Charts: 10 weeks; top spot no. 52
》**No. 310** *from Rolling Stone® Magazine's 500 Greatest Songs of All Time*

When an industrial accident left guitarist Tony Iommi without the tips of two of his fingers, it seemed like death for Black Sabbath. But he fashioned replacements out of pieces of a bottle and developed a playing style that would yield the riff that would define heavy metal forever.

***Appears on: Paranoid** (Warner Bros.)*

(Music appears on page 198)

Kashmir
Led Zeppelin

Written by: John Bonham, Jimmy Page, Robert Plant
Produced by: Page
Released: March '75 on Swan Song
Charts: non-single
》**No. 140** *from Rolling Stone® Magazine's 500 Greatest Songs of All Time*

While vacationing in southern Morocco, Plant conjured the lyrics for Led Zeppelin's most ambitious experiment, the centerpiece of 1975's *Physical Graffiti*. As he traveled the desert in northwest Africa, Plant envisioned himself driving straight through to Kashmir. Meanwhile, back in the band's studio in rural England, Page and Bonham began riffing on an Arabic-sounding set of chords that would perfectly match Plant's desert vision.

John Paul Jones' string arrangement provided the crowning touch, ratcheting up the song's mystic grandeur to stadium-rock proportion.

Appears on: Physical Graffiti (Atlantic)

(Music appears on page 204)

Killing Me Softly With His Song
Roberta Flack

Written by: Norman Gimbel, Charles Fox
Produced by: Joel Dorn
Released: Jan. '73 on Atlantic
Charts: 16 weeks; top spot no. 1
»**No. 360** *from Rolling Stone® Magazine's 500 Greatest Songs of All Time*

Inspired by a Don McLean gig at L.A.'s Troubadour, folk singer Lori Lieberman jotted down the idea for the song, then took it to Gimbel and Fox (of *Happy Days* fame). Flack heard Lieberman's recording on an in-flight radio station and "absolutely freaked," she said. She tracked down the songwriters, then spent three months in the studio with Dorn perfecting the track.

Appears on: Killing Me Softly (Atlantic)

(Music appears on page 216)

Knocking on Heaven's Door
Bob Dylan

Written by: Dylan
Produced by: Gordon Carroll
Released: July '73 on Columbia
Charts: 16 weeks; top spot no. 12
»**No. 190** *from Rolling Stone® Magazine's 500 Greatest Songs of All Time*

Three years had passed since his last studio album, and Dylan seemed at a loss. So he accepted an invitation to go to Mexico for Sam Peckinpah's *Pat Garrett and Billy the Kid*, for which he shot a bit part and did the soundtrack. For a death scene, Dylan delivered this tale of a dying sheriff, who wants only to lay his "guns in the ground."

Appears on: The Essential Bob Dylan (Sony)

(Music appears on page 222)

Layla
Derek and the Dominos

Written by: Eric Clapton, Jim Gordon
Produced by: Tom Dowd and the Dominos
Released: Nov. '70 on Atco
Charts: 15 weeks; top spot no. 10
»**No. 27** *from Rolling Stone® Magazine's 500 Greatest Songs of All Time*

Embroiled in a love triangle with George and Patti Boyd Harrison, Clapton took the title for his greatest song from the Persian love story "Layla and Majnoun." Recorded by Derek and the Dominos – a short-lived ensemble that matched Clapton with members of Delaney and Bonnie's band – "Layla" storms with aching vocals and crosscutting riffs from Clapton and contributing guitarist Duane Allman, then dissolves into a serene, piano-based coda. "It was the heaviest thing going on at the time," Clapton told *Rolling Stone* in 1974. "That's what I wanted to write about most of all."

Appears on: Layla and Other Assorted Love Songs (Polydor)

(Music appears on page 225)

Like a Prayer
Madonna

Written by: Madonna, Patrick Leonard
Produced by: Madonna, Leonard
Released: March '89 on Sire
Charts: 16 weeks; top spot no. 1
»**No. 300** *from Rolling Stone® Magazine's 500 Greatest Songs of All Time*

Madonna sang "Like a Prayer" in a voice full of Catholic angst and disco thunder. It was her big personal statement as she turned thirty and closed the book on her first marriage. "I didn't have the censors on me in terms of emotions or music," Madonna said. "I did take a lot more chances with this one, but obviously success gives you the confidence to do those things." The obligatory controversial video featured burning crosses, black lingerie and masturbation in church.

Appears on: Like a Prayer (Warner Bros.)

(Music appears on page 232)

Lola
The Kinks

Written by: Ray Davies
Produced by: Davies
Released: Aug. '70 on Reprise
Charts: 14 weeks; top spot no. 9
»**No. 422** *from Rolling Stone® Magazine's 500 Greatest Songs of All Time*

The real Lola? Perhaps transvestite Candy Darling, whom Davies dated. "It was the stubble that gave it away," Ray said.

Appears on: *Lola Versus Powerman and the Moneygoround, Part One* *(Warner Bros.)*

(Music appears on page 240)

Losing My Religion
R.E.M.

Written by: Berry, Buck, Mills, Stipe
Produced by: Scott Litt, R.E.M.
Released: March '91 on Warner Bros.
Charts: 21 weeks; top spot no. 4
»**No. 169** *from Rolling Stone® Magazine's 500 Greatest Songs of All Time*

"Losing My Religion" is built around acoustic guitar and mandolin, not exactly a familiar sound on pop radio in the early Nineties – singer Michael Stipe called it a "freak hit." As for the subject matter, it's not religion: "I wanted to write a classic obsession song," he said. "So I did."

Appears on: *Out of Time* *(Warner Bros.)*

(Music appears on page 246)

Maggie May
Rod Stewart

Written by: Stewart, Martin Quittenton
Produced by: Stewart
Released: June '71 on Mercury
Charts: 17 weeks; top spot no. 1
»**No. 130** *from Rolling Stone® Magazine's 500 Greatest Songs of All Time*

Stewart plays a schoolboy in love with an older temptress in "Maggie May," trying desperately to subdue his hormones with common sense. The song was a last-minute addition to the LP *Every Picture Tells a Story* and was initially the B side of "Reason to Believe." Stewart has joked that if a DJ hadn't flipped the single over, he'd have gone back to his old job: digging graves. But the song's rustic country mandolin and acoustic guitars – and Mickey Waller's simple but relentless drum-bashing – were undeniable.

Appears on: *Every Picture Tells a Story* *(Mercury/Universal)*

(Music appears on page 252)

The Message
Grandmaster Flash and the Furious Five

Written by: Duke Bootee, Melle Mel
Produced by: Sylvia Robinson
Released: May '82 on Sugar Hill
Charts: 7 weeks; top spot no. 62
»**No. 51** *from Rolling Stone® Magazine's 500 Greatest Songs of All Time*

"The Message" was a breakthrough in hip-hop, taking the music from party anthems to street-level ghetto blues. It began as a poem by schoolteacher Bootee; Sugar Hill boss Robinson decided to make it a rap record with Melle Mel of the Furious Five. Said Flash in 1997, "I hated the fact that it was advertised as Grandmaster Flash and the Furious Five, because the only people on the record were Mel and Duke Bootee." But the song became an instant sensation on New York's hip-hop radio. "It played all day, every day," Flash said. "It put us on a whole new level."

Appears on: *The Best of Sugar Hill Records* *(Rhino)*

(Music appears on page 256)

Moondance
Van Morrison

Written by: Morrison
Produced by: Morrison
Released: Feb. '70 on Warner Bros.
Charts: 4 weeks; top spot no. 92
≫**No. 226** *from Rolling Stone® Magazine's 500 Greatest Songs of All Time*

The title song of Morrison's first self-produced album started "as a saxophone solo," he said. "I used to play this sax number over and over, anytime I picked up my horn." He played the sax solo on this recording, which combined the bucolic charm of his life in Woodstock, New York ("the cover of October skies"), with his love of the sophisticated jazz and R&B of Mose Allison and Ray Charles.

Appears on: Moondance *(Warner Bros.)*

(Music appears on page 262)

No Woman, No Cry
Bob Marley and the Wailers

Written by: Vincent Ford, Marley
Produced by: Chris Blackwell, Marley and the Wailers
Released: May '75 on Island
Charts: did not chart
≫**No. 37** *from Rolling Stone® Magazine's 500 Greatest Songs of All Time*

The "government yard in Trench Town" refers to the Jamaican public-housing project where Marley lived in the late Fifties. Marley gave a songwriting credit on "No Woman, No Cry" to childhood friend Vincent "Tata" Ford in order to help keep Ford's Kingston soup kitchen running.

Appears on: Natty Dread *(Island)*

(Music appears on page 267)

O-o-h Child
The Five Stairsteps

Written by: Stan Vincent
Produced by: Vincent
Released: April '70 on Buddah
Charts: 16 weeks; top spot no. 8
≫**No. 392** *from Rolling Stone® Magazine's 500 Greatest Songs of All Time*

"O-o-h Child" gave the Five Stairsteps – four brothers and a sister from Chicago – a pop-soul classic that rivaled the hits of another sibling gang, the Jackson 5. The children of police detective Clarence Burke, the Five Stairsteps, who played their own music as well as sang, ranged in age from thirteen to seventeen when Curtis Mayfield signed them to his Windy C label.

Appears on:
Soul Hits of the '70s: Didn't It Blow Your Mind! Vol. 2 *(Rhino)*

(Music appears on page 274)

Paranoid
Black Sabbath

Written by: Geezer Butler, Tony Iommi, Ozzy Osbourne, William Ward
Produced by: Rodger Bain
Released: Nov. '70 on Warner Bros.
Charts: 8 weeks; top spot no. 61
≫**No. 250** *from Rolling Stone® Magazine's 500 Greatest Songs of All Time*

After Sabbath's first U.S. tour, guitarist Tony Iommi hunkered down at Regent Studios in London, trying to write one more song for the group's second album. "I started fiddling about on the guitar and came up with this riff," he said. "When the others came back [from lunch], we recorded it on the spot." "Paranoid," a two-minute blast of protopunk, became Sabbath's biggest single. It is also proof of the short distance between heavy metal and the Ramones.

Appears on: Paranoid *(Castle)*

(Music appears on page 279)

Paranoid Android
Radiohead

Written by: Thom Yorke
Produced by: Nigel Godrich, Radiohead
Released: May '97 on Capitol
Charts: did not chart
» No. 256 *from Rolling Stone® Magazine's 500 Greatest Songs of All Time*

"'Paranoid Android' is about the dullest fucking people on earth," said singer Yorke, referring to lyrics such as "Squealing Gucci little piggy," about a creepy coked-out woman he once spied at an L.A. bar. The sound was just as unnerving: a shape-shifting, three-part prog-rock suite. Spooky fact: It was recorded in actress Jane Seymour's fifteenth-century mansion, a house that Yorke was convinced was haunted.

Appears on: OK Computer (Capitol)

(Music appears on page 284)

Personality Crisis
New York Dolls

Written by: David Johansen, Johnny Thunders
Produced by: Todd Rundgren
Released: Aug. '73 on Mercury
Charts: did not chart
» No. 267 *from Rolling Stone® Magazine's 500 Greatest Songs of All Time*

No song better captured the New York Dolls' glammed-out R&B than "Personality Crisis," the opening track on the group's debut album. Produced by Rundgren during an eight-day session, "Personality Crisis" was the trashy sound of an identity meltdown. Soon after, the Dolls fell victim to one themselves and dissolved amid a haze of drugs.

Appears on: New York Dolls (Mercury)

(Music appears on page 291)

Ramble On
Led Zeppelin

Written by: Jimmy Page, Robert Plant
Produced by: Page
Released: Oct. '69 on Atlantic
Charts: non-single
» No. 433 *from Rolling Stone® Magazine's 500 Greatest Songs of All Time*

Groupies and "The Lord of the Rings" seemed to provide the inspiration for "Ramble On," recorded in 1969 in New York on Led Zeppelin's first U.S. tour. Over Page's acoustic guitars, Plant wails, "In the darkest depths of Mordor/I met a girl so fair." Middle-Earth influenced more than just the band's music: "After reading Tolkien," Page said, "I knew I had to move to the country." Legend has it that John Bonham plays a plastic garbage can on the song.

Appears on: Led Zeppelin II (Atlantic)

(Music appears on page 300)

Rapper's Delight
Sugarhill Gang

Written by: S. Robinson, H. Jackson, M. Wright, G. O'Brien
Produced by: Sylvia Robinson
Released: Oct. '79 on Sugar Hill
Charts: 12 weeks; top spot no. 36
» No. 248 *from Rolling Stone® Magazine's 500 Greatest Songs of All Time*

Master Gee, Wonder Mike and Big Bank Hank were a pure studio creation, a trio of unknown MCs recruited by Sugar Hill's Sylvia Robinson to make rap's first radio hit. Based on a sample of Chic's "Good Times," the track – with raps about bad food instead of boasting – kept going hip-hop, hippity-to-the-hop for fifteen minutes.

Appears on:
Rapper's Delight: The Best of Sugarhill Gang (Rhino)

(Music appears on page 305)

Redemption Song
Bob Marley and the Wailers

Written by: Marley
Produced by: Chris Blackwell
Released: June '80 on Island
Charts: did not chart
» No. 66 *from Rolling Stone® Magazine's 500 Greatest Songs of All Time*

Marley had already recorded a version of this freedom hymn with his band when Island Records' Blackwell suggested he try it as an acoustic-style folk tune. Inspired by the writings of Marcus

Garvey, Marley's lyrics offer up music as an antidote to slavery, both mental and physical. "I would love to do more like that," Marley said a few months before his death in 1981. The song might have signaled a new direction for his work; instead, as the final track on his final album, it's his epitaph.

Appears on: Uprising (Island)

(Music appears on page 308)

Running On Empty
Jackson Browne

Written by: Browne
Produced by: Browne
Released: Jan. '77 on Asylum
Charts: 17 weeks; top spot no. 11
≫No. 492 *from Rolling Stone® Magazine's 500 Greatest Songs of All Time*

"Running On Empty" was Browne's grand experiment: a live album of all-new songs recorded onstage, in hotel rooms and on the tour bus. The title track was actually written when Browne was driving back and forth to the studio each day to make *The Pretender*. "I was always driving around with no gas in the car," he said. "I just never bothered to fill up the tank because – how far was it anyway? Just a few blocks."

Appears on: Running On Empty (Elektra)

(Music appears on page 312)

Sail Away
Randy Newman

Written by: Newman
Produced by: Lenny Waronker
Released: June '72 on Reprise
Charts: did not chart
≫No. 264 *from Rolling Stone® Magazine's 500 Greatest Songs of All Time*

Everybody from Ray Charles to Etta James has covered this piano ballad – even though it's a portrait of America from the perspective of a slave trader. As usual for Newman, it combines lush melody with painfully funny satire. "One thing with my music," Newman admitted, "you can't sit and eat potato chips and have it on in the background at a party."

Appears on: Sail Away (Rhino)

(Music appears on page 320)

Stairway to Heaven
Led Zeppelin

Written by: Jimmy Page, Robert Plant
Produced by: Page
Released: Nov. '71 on Atlantic
Charts: non-single
≫No. 31 *from Rolling Stone® Magazine's 500 Greatest Songs of All Time*

All epic anthems must measure themselves against "Stairway to Heaven," the cornerstone of *Led Zeppelin IV*. Building from an acoustic intro that sounds positively Elizabethan, thanks to John Paul Jones' recorder solo and Plant's fanciful lyrics, it morphs into a Page solo that storms heaven's gate. Page said the song "crystallized the essence of the band. It had everything there and showed the band at its best.... as a band, as a unit.... It was a milestone for us. Every musician wants to do something of lasting quality, something which will hold up for a long time, and I guess we did it with 'Stairway.'"

Appears on: Led Zeppelin IV (Atlantic)

(Music appears on page 334)

Stayin' Alive
Bee Gees

Written by: Robin Gibb, Barry Gibb, Maurice Gibb
Produced by: Barry Gibb, Robin Gibb, Maurice Gibb, Karl Richardson, Albhy Galuten
Released: Nov. '77 on RSO
Charts: 27 weeks; top spot no. 1
≫No. 189 *from Rolling Stone® Magazine's 500 Greatest Songs of All Time*

This disco classic was written after Robert Stigwood asked the Bee Gees for music for a film he was producing based on a *New York* magazine account of the Brooklyn club scene.

Appears on: Saturday Night Fever (Polydor)

(Music appears on page 344)

Sweet Child O' Mine
Guns n' Roses

Written by: Guns n' Roses
Produced by: Mike Clink
Released: Aug. '87 on Geffen
Charts: 24 weeks; top spot no. 1
»No. 196 *from Rolling Stone® Magazine's 500 Greatest Songs of All Time*

In the midst of an album full of songs about cheap drugs and cheaper sex came Axl Rose's love letter to his girlfriend, Erin Everly (daughter of Don Everly). Slash has said he was just "fucking around with the intro riff, making a joke"; neither he nor the rest of the band thought much of it, but Rose knew better. Rose and Erin Everly were later married – for all of one month.

Appears on: Appetite for Destruction (Geffen)
(Music appears on page 350)

Thank You (Falettinme Be Mice Elf Agin)
Sly and the Family Stone

Written by: Sylvester Stewart
Produced by: Stewart
Released: Jan. '70 on Epic
Charts: 13 weeks; top spot no. 1
»No. 402 *from Rolling Stone® Magazine's 500 Greatest Songs of All Time*

"Thank You" rode on the finger-popping bass of Larry Graham, who came up with the technique in a duo with his organist mother. "I started to thump the strings with my thumb," he said, "to make up for not having a drummer."

Appears on: Anthology (Epic)
(Music appears on page 358)

Thunder Road
Bruce Springsteen

Written by: Bruce Springsteen
Produced by: Springsteen, Jon Landau, Mike Appel
Released: Aug. '75 on Columbia
Charts: non-single
»No. 86 *from Rolling Stone® Magazine's 500 Greatest Songs of All Time*

"We decided to make a guitar album, but then I wrote all the songs on piano," Springsteen said of his third album, *Born to Run*. "Thunder Road," its opening track, is a cinematic tale of redemption with a title borrowed from a 1958 hillbilly noir starring Robert Mitchum as a bootlegger with a car that can't be beat. These days, with Springsteen in his midfifties, he marvels that he wrote the line "You're scared, and you're thinking that maybe we ain't that young any more" when he was all of twenty-four years old.

Appears on: Born to Run (Columbia)
(Music appears on page 325)

Walk on the Wild Side
Lou Reed

Written by: Reed
Produced by: David Bowie, Mick Ronson, Reed
Released: Dec. '72 on RCA
Charts: 14 weeks; top spot no. 16
»No. 221 *from Rolling Stone® Magazine's 500 Greatest Songs of All Time*

After Reed left the Velvet Underground in 1970, he was asked to write songs for a musical based on Nelson Algren's novel *A Walk on the Wild Side*. The show was never mounted, but Reed kept the title and applied it to characters he knew from Andy Warhol's Factory. "I always thought it would be kinda fun to introduce people you see at parties but don't dare approach," said Reed.

Appears on: Transformer (RCA)
(Music appears on page 364)

What's Going On
Marvin Gaye

Written by: Gaye, Renaldo Benson, Al Cleveland
Produced by: Gaye
Released: Feb. '71 on Tamla
Charts: 13 weeks; top spot no. 2
»No. 4 *from Rolling Stone® Magazine's 500 Greatest Songs of All Time*

"What's Going On" is an exquisite plea for peace on earth, sung by a man at the height of crisis. In 1970, Marvin Gaye was Motown's top male vocal star, yet he was frustrated by the assembly-line role he played on his own hits. Devastated by the loss of duet partner Tammi Terrell, who died that March after a three-year battle with a brain tumor, Gaye was also trapped in a turbulent marriage to Anna Gordy, Motown boss Berry Gordy's sister. Gaye was tormented, too, by his relationship with his puritanical father, Marvin Sr. "If I was arguing for peace," Gaye told biographer David Ritz, "I knew I'd have to find peace in my heart."

Not long after Terrell's passing, Renaldo Benson of the Four Tops presented Gaye with a song he had written with Motown staffer Al Cleveland. Benson later claimed that he gave Gaye a co-writing credit as an inducement to sing and produce the track. But Gaye made the song his own: directly overseeing the liquid beauty of David Van DePitte's arrangement (although Gaye could not read or write music) and investing the topical references to war and racial strife with private anguish. Motown session crew the Funk Brothers cut the stunning, jazz-inflected rhythm track, which was unlike anything in the label's Sixties hit parade (Gaye played cardboard-box percussion). Then Gaye invoked his own family in moving prayer: singing to his younger brother Frankie, a Vietnam veteran ("Brother, brother, brother/ There's far too many of you dying"), and appealing for calm closer to home ("Father, father, father/We don't need to escalate").

Initially rejected as uncommercial, "What's Going On" (with background vocals by two players from the Detroit Lions) was Gaye's finest studio achievement, a timeless gift of healing. But for Gaye, the peace he craved never came: On April 1st, 1984, he died in a family dispute – shot by his father.

Appears on: What's Going On (Tamla)

(Music appears on page 368)

Wild Horses
The Rolling Stones

Written by: Mick Jagger, Keith Richards
Produced by: Jimmy Miller
Released: April '71 on Rolling Stones
Charts: 8 weeks; top spot no. 28
»No. 334 *from Rolling Stone® Magazine's 500 Greatest Songs of All Time*

Richards wrote this acoustic ballad about leaving his wife Anita and young son Marlon as the Stones prepared for their first American tour in three years. Stones sidekick Ian Stewart refused to play the minor chords required, so Memphis musical maverick Jim Dickinson filled in on upright piano at the Muscle Shoals, Alabama, recording session for *Sticky Fingers*.

Appears on: Sticky Fingers (Virgin)

(Music appears on page 373)

Wish You Were Here
Pink Floyd

Written by: David Gilmour, Roger Waters
Produced by: Pink Floyd
Released: Sept. '75 on Columbia
Charts: non-single
»No. 316 *from Rolling Stone® Magazine's 500 Greatest Songs of All Time*

While Pink Floyd were recording this elegy for burned-out ex-frontman Syd Barrett, he mysteriously appeared in the studio in such bad shape nobody recognized him. "He stood up and said, 'Right, when do I put my guitar on?'" keyboardist Rick Wright recalled. "And of course, he didn't have a guitar with him. And we said, 'Sorry, Syd, the guitar's all done.'"

Appears on: Wish You Were Here (Capitol)

(Music appears on page 378)

ANOTHER BRICK IN THE WALL PART 2

Words and Music by
ROGER WATERS

Moderately ♩ = 108

Verse:

1. We don't need__ no ed - u - ca - tion.
2. We don't need__ no ed - u - ca - tion.

We don't need__ no thought con - trol.__
We don't need__ no thought con - trol.__

No dark sar - cas - ms in the class - rooms.
No dark sar - cas - ms in the class - rooms.

Another Brick in the Wall Part 2 - 4 - 1

Another Brick in the Wall Part 2 - 4 - 4

BEAT IT

Written and Composed by
MICHAEL JACKSON

1. They told him, "Don't you ev - er come a - round here. Don't wan - na see your face; you bet - ter
2. They're out to get you. Bet - ter leave while you can. Don't wan - na be a boy; you wan - na
3. *Guitar solo ad lib.*

*Original recording sounds a half step lower than written.

Beat It - 5 - 1

26

BIZARRE LOVE TRIANGLE

Words and Music by
STEPHEN MORRIS, PETER HOOK,
BERNARD SUMNER and GILLIAN GILBERT

Moderately ♩ = 116

N.C.

mf

Verse:

1. Ev - 'ry___ time I think of you,___ I feel
2. I feel___ fine and I feel good.___

shot right through with a bolt of blue.___ It's no
I'm feel - ing like I nev - er should.___ When - ev - er

Bizarre Love Triangle - 7 - 1

Chorus:

Ev - 'ry time I see___ you fall - ing, I get down on my knees___ and pray.___ I'm wait - ing for the fi - nal mo - ment you___ say the words that I___ can't say.___

nal mo - ment you_____ say the words that I_____ can't say._____

N.C.

sim.

(Inst. solo ad lib....

(Cont. Inst. solo ad lib.)

BILLIE JEAN

Written and Composed by
MICHAEL JACKSON

kid___ is not my son.___

(Guitar:)

She says I___ am the one.___ but the

BITTER SWEET SYMPHONY

Words and Music by
MICK JAGGER, KEITH RICHARDS
and RICHARD ASHCROFT

BLACK DOG

Words and Music by
JIMMY PAGE, ROBERT PLANT
and JOHN PAUL JONES

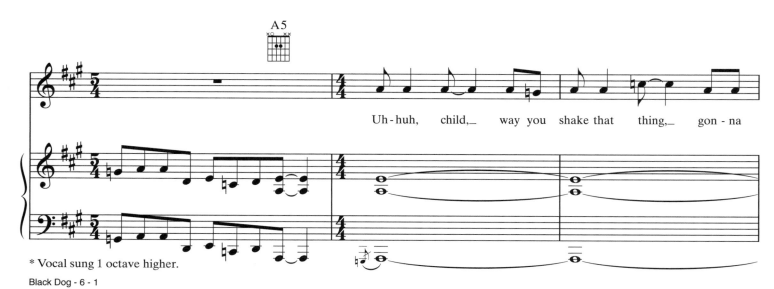

* Vocal sung 1 octave higher.

Black Dog - 6 - 1

Chorus:

yeah, oh___ yeah, ah___ ah___ ah.___ Oh__

Verses 2 & 4:

2. I got - ta roll, can't stand still,___ got a flam - in' heart,___ can't
4. *See additional lyrics*

get my fill.___

N.C.

cue notes 2nd time only

Eyes that shine,___ burn - in' red,___ dreams of you___ all

Verse 3:
Didn't take too long 'fore I found out what
People mean by down and out.

Spent my money, took my car ,
Started tellin' her friends she gonna be a star.

I don't know, but I been told,
A big-legged woman ain't got no soul.
(To Chorus:)

Verse 4:
All I ask for, all I pray,
Steady loaded woman gonna come my way.

Need a woman gonna hold my hand
Will tell me no lies, make me a happy man.
Ah ah ah ah ah ah ah ah ah ah ah ah ah.
(To Coda)

BLITZKRIEG BOP

Words and Music by
JEFFREY HYMAN, JOHN CUMMINGS,
DOUGLAS COLVIN and THOMAS ERDELYI

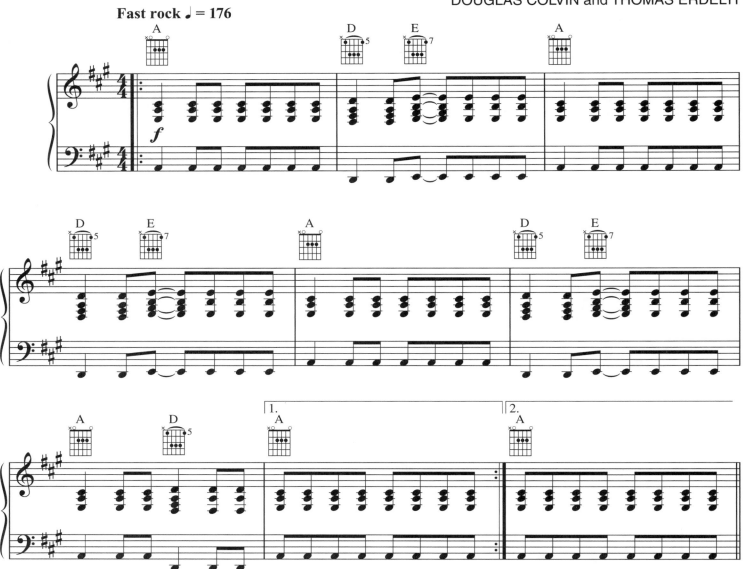

BOHEMIAN RHAPSODY

Words and Music by
FREDDY MERCURY

mor-row, car-ry on, car-ry on, as if noth-ing real - ly mat-ters.

all. (Guitar solo)

Be - el - ze - bub has a dev - il put a - side for

mi - a, let me go! Be - el - ze - bub has a dev - il put a - side for

me, _____ for me, _____ for me! _____

me, for me, for me! _____

With a heavy rock beat

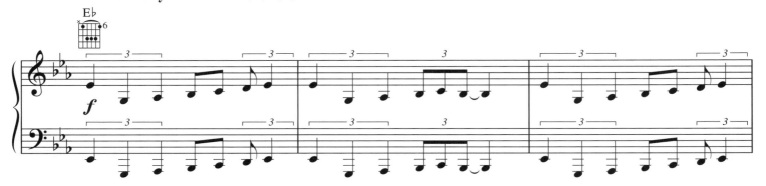

BORN IN THE U.S.A.

Words and Music by
BRUCE SPRINGSTEEN

Moderately ♩ = 120

Verses 1–3:

1. Born down in a dead man's_ town,_ the first kick I took was when I
2.3. *See additional lyrics*

hit the ground._____ End up like a dog that's been beat too___ much,_ till you spend_

Chorus:

Verses 4–6:

4. I had a broth-er at Khe Sanh,___ fight-in' off the
5.6. *See additional lyrics*

Vi - et - cong;_____ they're still there, he's all__ gone._____

1.2. ‖ *3.*

no-where to go._____

Chorus:

Born in the U. S.__ A.__ I was born in the

Repeat ad lib. and fade

Verse 2:
Got in a little hometown jam,
So they put a rifle in my hand.
Sent me off to a foreign land
To go and kill the yellow man.
(To Chorus:)

Verse 3:
Come back to the refinery;
Hiring man says, "Son, if it was up to me."
Went down to see my V.A. man; he said,
"Son, don't you understand, now?"
(To Instrumental Chorus:)

Verse 5:
He had a woman that he loved in Saigon,
I got a picture of him in her arms, now.

Verse 6:
Down in the shadow of the penitentiary.
Out by the gas fires of the refinery;
I'm ten years burning down the road,
Nowhere to run, ain't got nowhere to go.
(To Chorus:)

BORN TO RUN

Words and Music by
BRUCE SPRINGSTEEN

Moderately fast ♩ = 144

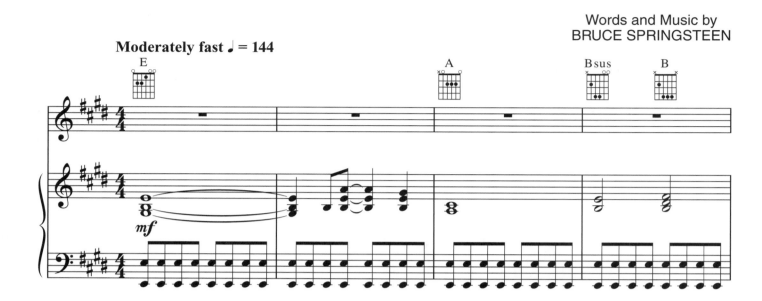

Verses 1 & 2:

day we sweat it out___ on the streets of a run-a-way A-mer-i-can dream.___
let me in, I wan-na be your friend, I wan-na guard your dreams and vi-sions.___

Born to Run - 10 - 1

Bridge:

yond the Pal - ace, hem - i - pow-ered drones_ scream_ down the bou - le - vard._

_____ Girls comb their hair_ in rear - view mir - rors and the

boys try to look so hard. The a - muse-ment park_ ris - es

bold and stark_ as kids are hud-dled on the beach in the mist._____ I wan - na

die with you, Wen-dy, on the streets to-night___ in an ev-er-last-ing kiss.___ *Huh!*

One, two three, four! 3. The

Verse 3:

E A

high-way's jammed_ with bro - ken he - ros on a last - chance pow-er drive.

Bsus B E

Ev - 'ry - bod - y's out on the run____ to-night, but there's

A Bsus B A

no place left to hide.____ To - geth - er, Wen - dy, we can

BRIDGE OVER TROUBLED WATER

Words and Music by
PAUL SIMON

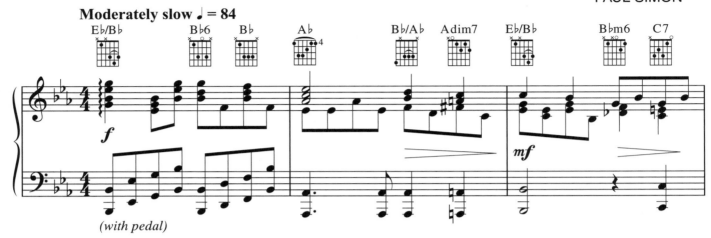

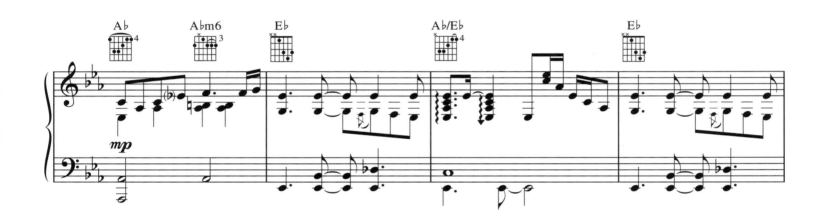

Verse 1:

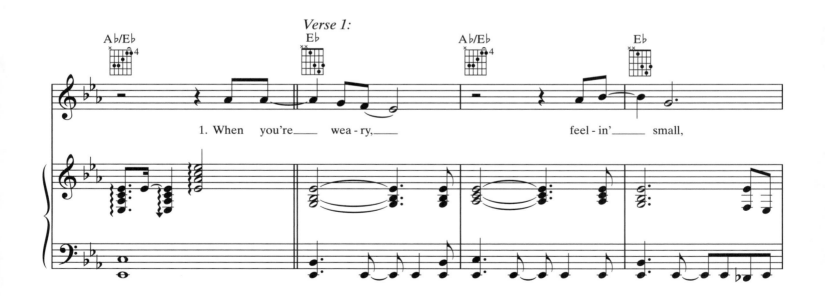

1. When you're___ wea - ry,___ feel - in'___ small,

Verse 2:

down and out,__ when you're on the street,

when eve - ning falls so hard,_____ I will

com - fort_ you._____ I'll take your

part,_____ oh,_____ when dark - ness comes,__

THE BOYS OF SUMMER

Words and Music by
DON HENLEY and MIKE CAMPBELL

*Original recording in E♭ minor with guitar tuned down one half step.

The Boys of Summer - 5 - 1

Verse:

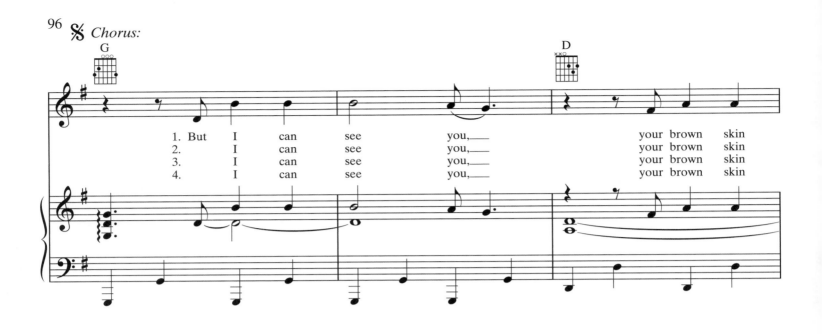

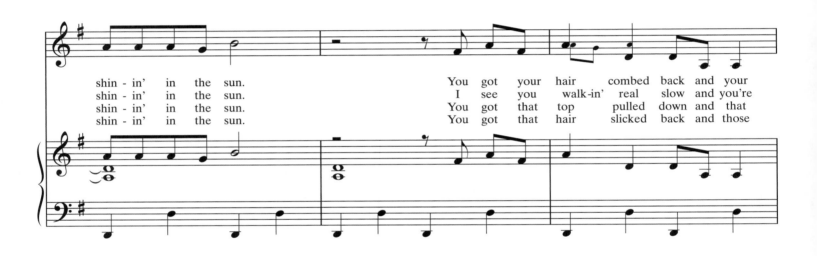

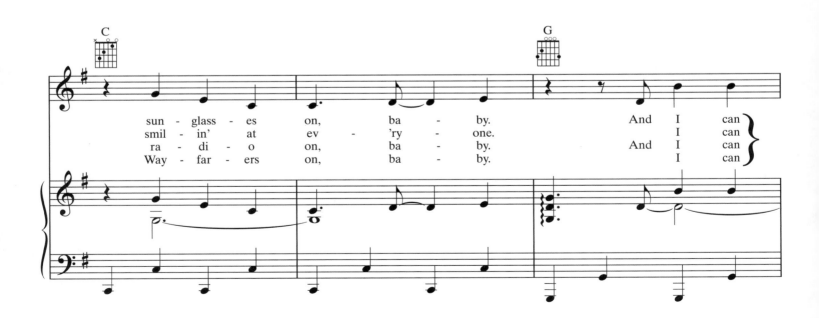

98

Verse 2:
I never will forget those nights. I wonder if it was a dream.
Remember how you made me crazy? Remember how I made you scream?
Now I don't understand what happened to our love.
But, babe, I'm gonna get you back. I'm gonna show you what I'm made of.
(To Chorus 2:)

Verse 3:
Out on the road today I saw a "Deadhead" sticker on a Cadillac.
A little voice inside my head said, "Don't look back. You can never look back."
I thought I knew what love was. What did I know?
Those days are gone forever. I should just let them go, but…
(To Chorus 3:)

COMFORTABLY NUMB

Words and Music by
ROGER WATERS and DAVID GILMOUR

Slowly ♩ = 66

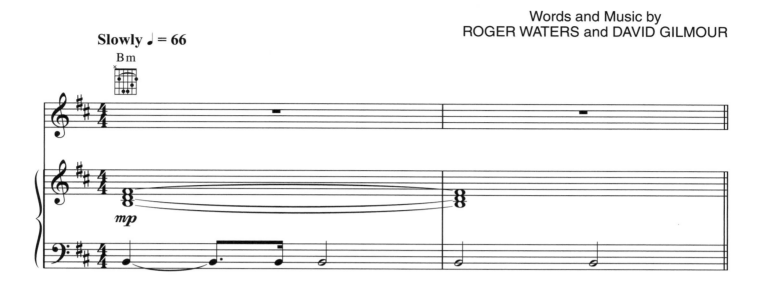

Verse:

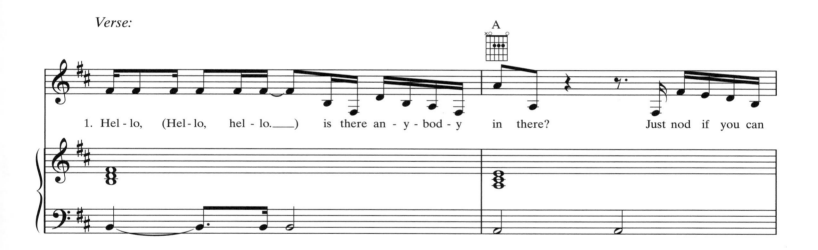

1. Hel - lo, (Hel - lo, hel - lo.___) is there an - y - bod - y in there? Just nod if you can

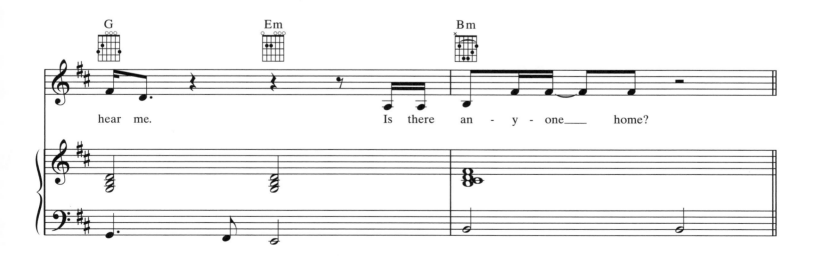

hear me. Is there an - y - one___ home?

Comfortably Numb - 5 - 1

Chorus:

DANCING QUEEN

Words and Music by
BENNY ANDERSSON, STIG ANDERSON
and BJORN ULVAEUS

Moderate disco beat ♩ = 104

DESPERADO

Words and Music by
DON HENLEY and GLENN FREY

rain-bow a - bove__ you. You bet - ter let some-bod-y love you,

you____ bet - ter let some - bod - y love____ you_____ be -

fore it's too_____ late.

mp

a tempo

rit.

FLASH LIGHT

Words and Music by
GEORGE CLINTON, BOOTSY COLLINS
and BERNARD WORRELL

Funk ♩ = 104

Now ___ I lay me down_ to sleep.___

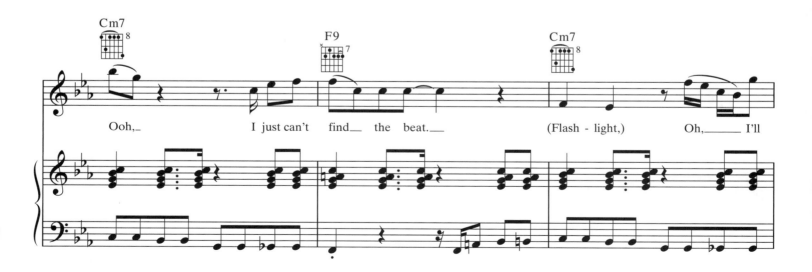

Ooh,___ I just can't find__ the beat.___ (Flash - light,) Oh,_____ I'll

Flash Light - 6 - 1

FREE FALLIN'

Words and Music by
TOM PETTY and JEFF LYNNE

HALLELUJAH

Words and Music by
LEONARD COHEN

Hallelujah - 8 - 1

1. Well, I heard there was___ a se-cret chord___ that
   faith was strong,___ but you need-ed proof.___ That You
   ba - by, I've___ been here be - fore,___ I've

Da - vid played___ and it pleased the Lord, but you don't___ real-ly care for mu - sic,
saw her bath - ing___ on the roof. Her beau - ty___ and the moon - light o - ver -
seen this room___ and I've walked this floor. I used to live a - lone be - fore I

do you?___ Well, it goes like this: The fourth, the fifth, the
threw you.___ Well, she tied you to her kitch - en chair, and she
knew you.___ And I've seen your flag on the mar - ble arch, and

mi - nor fall and the ma - jor lift.___ The baf - fled king,___ com - pos - ing Hal - le -
broke your throne, and she cut your hair,___ and from your lips,___ she drew the Hal - le -
love is not a vic - t'ry march,___ it's a cold and it's a bro - ken Hal - le -

5. Well,

Verse 5:

may-be there's_ a God a-bove,_ but all I've__ ev-er learned from love__ was

how to shoot some-bod-y who out-drew you._

And it's not a cry__ that you hear at night, it's

THE HARDER THEY COME

Words and Music by
JIMMY CLIFF

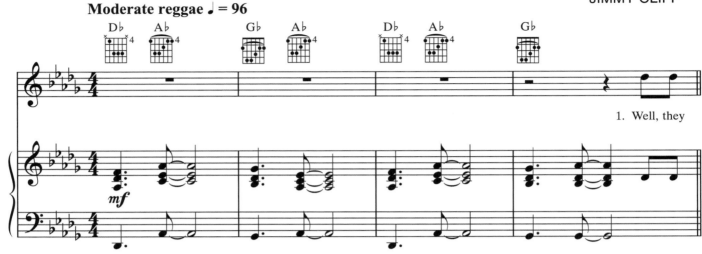

The Harder They Come - 4 - 1

Chorus:

FAKE PLASTIC TREES

Words and Music by
THOMAS YORKE, EDWARD O'BRIEN, COLIN GREENWOOD,
JONATHAN GREENWOOD and PHILIP SELWAY

Moderately slow ♩ = 76

Verses 1 & 2:

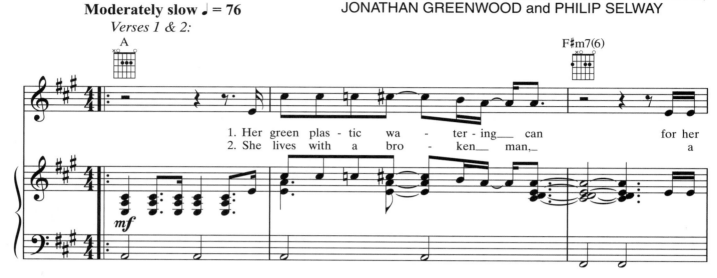

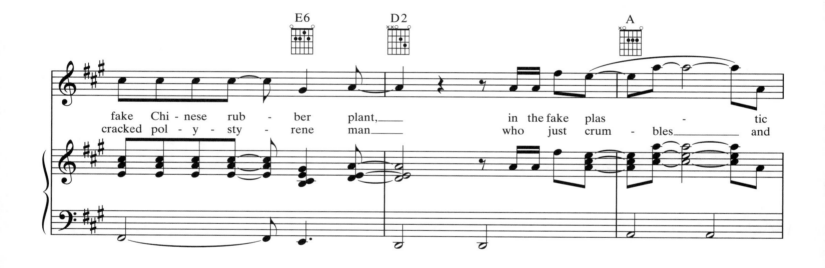

HEARTBREAKER

Words and Music by
JIMMY PAGE, ROBERT PLANT,
JOHN PAUL JONES and JOHN BONHAM

Moderately (♩ = 98)

way you call____ me an-oth-er guy's name when I try to make love to

you,____ yeah.____

N.C.

Freetime

* Optional guitar solo adapted for keyboards. (Sounds an octave lower.)
Use pitch bend and modulation controls to achieve desired effects.

Repeat as desired for solo

D.S. 𝄋 al Coda

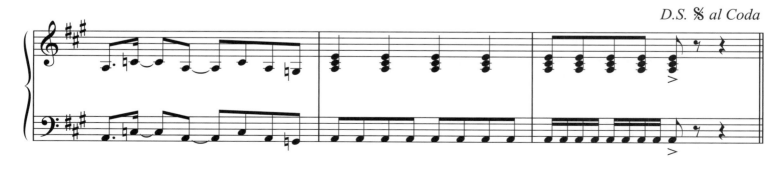

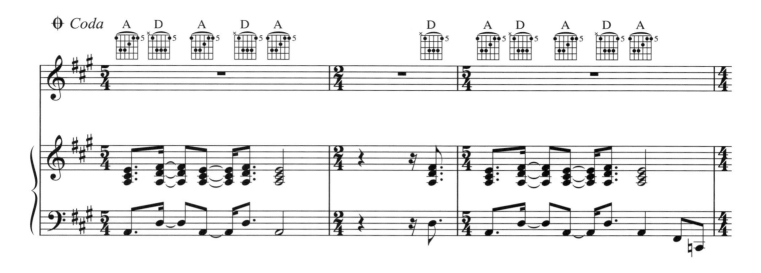

Heart - break - er!   Heart - break-er!   Heart!

Verse 2:
Well, it's been ten years and maybe more since I first set eyes on you.
The best years of my life gone by. Here I am alone and blue.
Some people cry and some people die by the wicked ways of love.
But I'll just keep rollin' along with the grace of the Lord above.

Verse 3:
Work so hard I can't unwind, get some money saved,
Abuse my love a thousand times, however hard I try.
Heartbreaker, your time has come, can't take your evil ways.
Go away, you heartbreaker.

HELP ME

Words and Music by
JONI MITCHELL

Moderate rock ♩ = 84

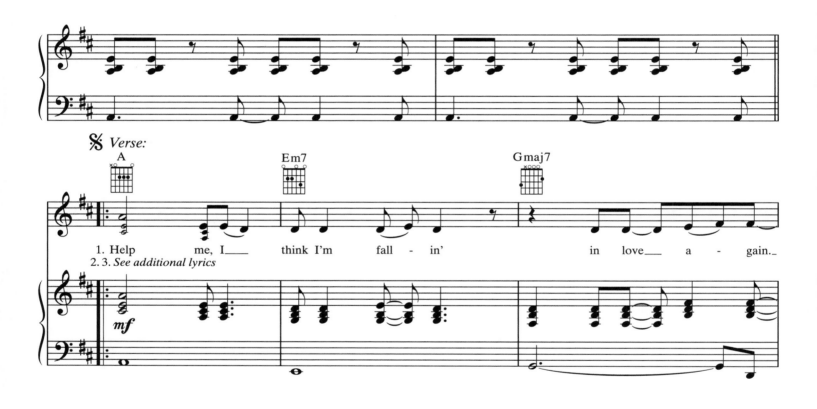

%Verse:

1. Help me, I___ think I'm fall - in' in love___ a - gain.___
2.3. *See additional lyrics*

When I get that cra - zy feel - in',___ I know___

Help Me - 6 - 1

I'm in trou-ble a - gain.__ I'm in trou - ble 'cause you're a

ram-bler and a gam-bler and a sweet-talk - in'__ la - dies__ man,__ and you

love_____ your lov - in',_____

but not like you love__ your__ free -

Bridge:

did-n't it feel good?_ We were sit-tin' there_ talk - in' or ly - in' there not__ talk - in'.

Did-n't it feel good?_ You danced with the la - dy with a hole in her stock - ing.

Did-n't it feel_____ good,_____ did-n't it_____

___ feel_____ good?____

(Bkgrd.) Did - n't it feel___ good?_

Did-n't it feel____ good?_ Did - n't it feel__
_ good?_ Did - n't it feel____ good?_

✆ *Coda*

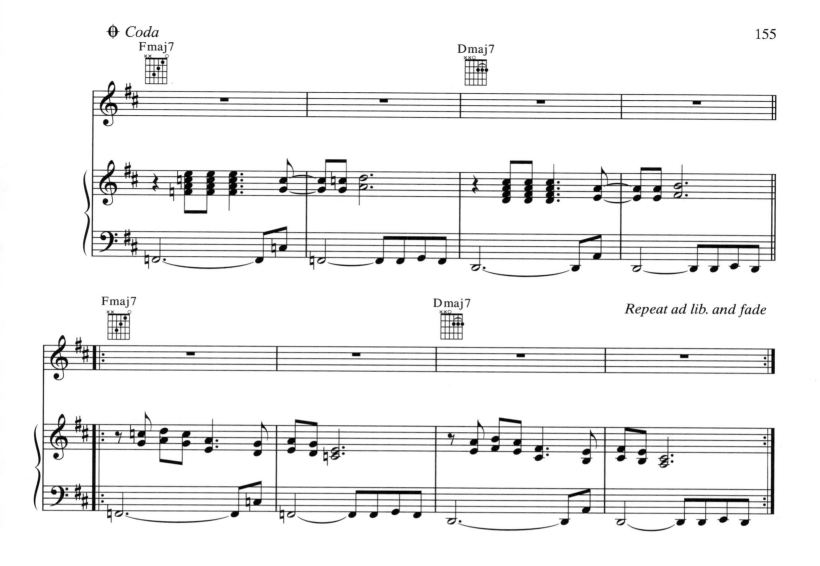

Repeat ad lib. and fade

Verse 2:
Help me, I think I'm fallin' in love too fast.
It's got me hoping for the future and worrying about the past,
'Cause I've seen some hot, hot blazes come down to smoke and ash.
We love our lovin', but not like we love our freedom.
(To Bridge:)

Verse 3:
Help me, I think I'm fallin' in love with you.
Are you gonna let me go there by myself? That's such a lonely thing to do,
Both of us flirting around, flirting and flirting, hurting too.
We love our lovin', but not like we love our freedom.
(To Coda)

HOT FUN IN THE SUMMERTIME

Words and Music by
SYLVESTER STEWART

Verse 1:

1. End of the spring___ and___ here___ she___ comes___ back.

Hi, hi, hi,

Hot Fun in the Summertime - 5 - 1

HOW DEEP IS YOUR LOVE

Words and Music by
BARRY GIBB, MAURICE GIBB
and ROBIN GIBB

162

HOTEL CALIFORNIA

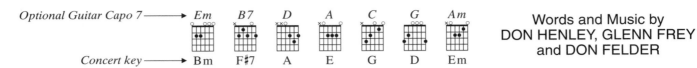

Words and Music by
DON HENLEY, GLENN FREY
and DON FELDER

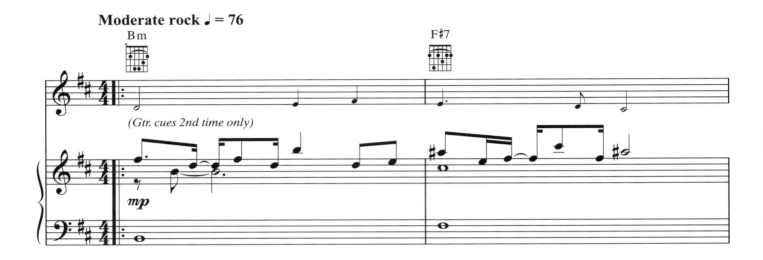

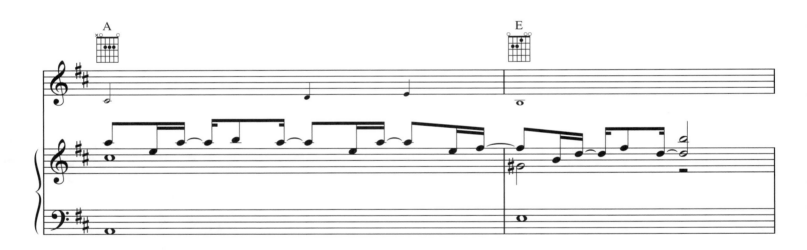

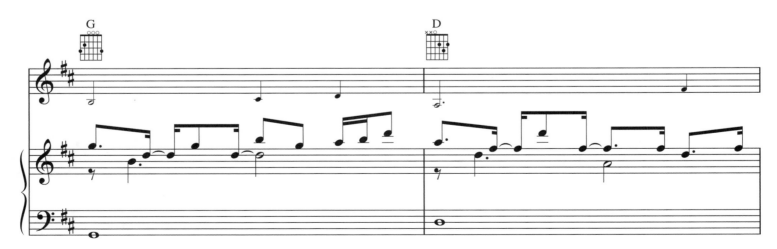

Hotel California - 8 - 1

Verses 1 & 2:

1. On a dark des-ert high-way, cool wind in my hair,
2. Her mind is Tif-fa-ny twist-ed, she got the Mer-ce-des Benz.

warm smell of co-li-tas rising up through the air.
She got a lot of pret-ty, pret-ty boys that she calls friends.

Up a-head in the dis-tance, I saw a shim-mer-ing light.
How they dance in the court-yard, sweet sum-mer sweat.

they gath-ered for the feast. They stab it____ with their steel-y knives,__ but they

just can't__ kill the beast. Last thing__ I re-mem-ber, I was

run-ning__ for the door. I had to find the pas-sage back__ to the

place I was__ be-fore._____ "Re-lax," said the night-man. "We are_

...end solo)

Repeat and fade

Hotel California - 8 - 8

HOW SOON IS NOW?

Moderately ♩ = 92

Words and Music by
STEVEN MORRISSEY
and JOHNNY MARR

Chorus 3:
There's a club if you'd like to go.
You could meet somebody who really loves you.
So you go and you stand on your own.
And you leave on your own, and you go home.
And you cry, and you want to die.

Chorus 4:
When you say it's gonna happen "now,"
Well, when exactly do you mean?
See, I've already waited too long,
And all my hope is gone.

Chorus 5:
(Instrumental)

I WANNA BE SEDATED

Words and Music by
JEFFREY HYMAN, JOHN CUMMINGS
and DOUGLAS COLVIN

Moderately fast ♩ = 160

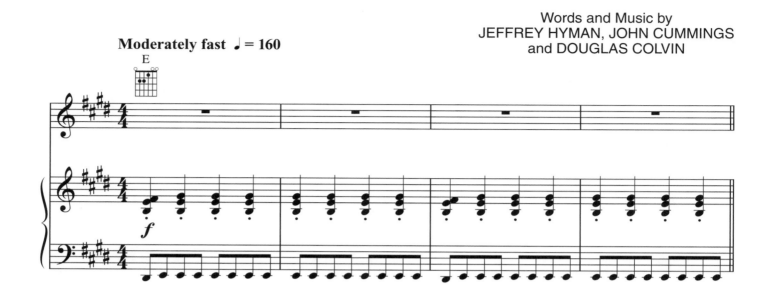

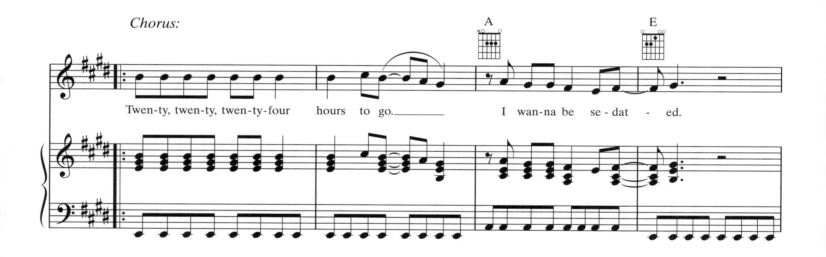

Chorus:

Twen-ty, twen-ty, twen-ty-four hours to go._____ I wan-na be se-dat-ed.

Noth-ing to do,___ no - where___ to go, ho.___ I wan-na be se-dat-ed. {Just / Just

I Wanna Be Sedated - 4 - 1

I WANT YOU BACK

Words and Music by
FREDDIE PERREN, ALPHONSO MIZELL,
BERRY GORDY and DEKE RICHARDS

Verse:

Chorus:

Repeat ad lib. and fade

I'LL TAKE YOU THERE

Words and Music by
ALVERTIS ISBELL

Moderately slow ♩ = 96

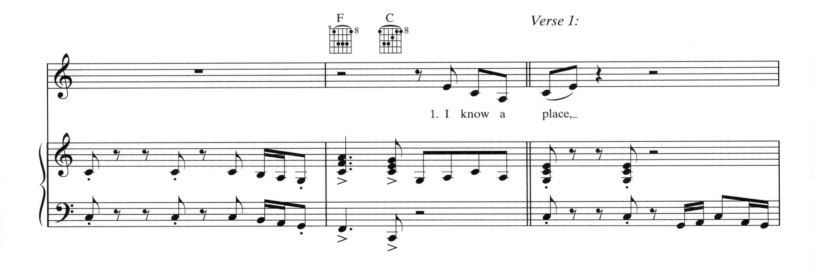

Verse 1:

1. I know a place,_

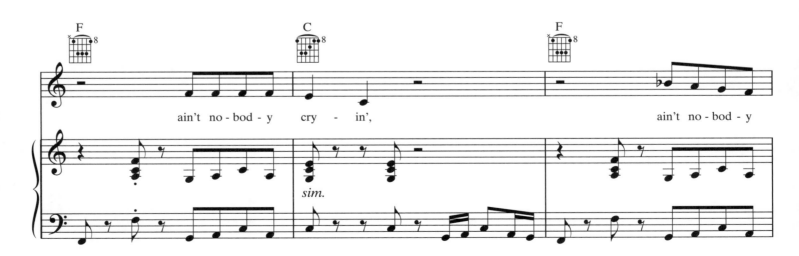

ain't no-bod-y cry-in',   ain't no-bod-y

sim.

I'll Take You There - 6 - 1

(Inst. solo ad lib....

sim.

|1. 2.|

|3.|

...end solos)

Verse 2:

2. I,_____ oh,_____ I,   I know___ a place, y'all, (I'll take you

190

INTO THE MYSTIC

Words and Music by
VAN MORRISON

We were born_____ be-fore the wind,

al - so young - er than the sun,

Into the Mystic - 6 - 1

And I re-mem-ber, sud-d'nly we will float in - to the
And to - geth - er we will float in - to the

mys - tic.
mys - tic.

Too late to stop now...

IRON MAN

Words and Music by
FRANK IOMMI, JOHN OSBOURNE,
WILLIAM WARD and TERENCE BUTLER

200

Iron Man - 6 - 3

that__ he will__ soon un - furl.____
now__ he has__ his re - venge.____

KASHMIR

Gtr. tuned in DADGAD
⑥ = D   ③ = G
⑤ = A   ② = A
④ = D   ① = D

Words and Music by
JIMMY PAGE, ROBERT PLANT
and JOHN BONHAM

Moderately ♩ = (80)

D5   Bb/D   D6(♭)   D7(♭)

mf

D5   D5   Bb/D   D6(♭)   D7(♭)

𝄋

D5   D5   Bb/D   D6(♭)

Oh, let the sun___ beat down up-on___ my face, with stars___ to

Oh, pi-lot of___ the storm who leaves___ no trace, like thoughts_ in-

D7(♭)   D5   D5   Bb/D

fill my dreams.___ I am a trav-'ler of both

side a dream,___ who hid the path_ that led me

Talk and songs_ from tongues of lilt-ing grace,___ whose sounds_ ca-
Oh, fa-ther of___ the four winds, fill my sails,___ a-cross___ the

Ooh_____ yes, I've been fly - ing._____

My___ Ma - ma, ain't

no de - ny - ing,_____ no de - ny - ing.

214

Kashmir - 12 - 11

KILLING ME SOFTLY WITH HIS SONG

Words and Music by
CHARLES FOX and NORMAN GIMBEL

Killing Me Softly With His Song - 6 - 1

words, kill-ing me soft - ly with his song.

A little faster ♩ = 120

Verse:

1. I heard he sang a good song,
2. I felt all flushed with fe - ver,
3. He sang as if he knew me,

Chorus:

strum-ming my pain,___ yeah,__ he was sing - ing my____ life.__

___ Kill - ing me soft - ly with his____ song, kill - ing me soft -

ly with his____ song, tell - ing my whole life with his____ words, kill - ing__

___ me___ soft - ly____ with his song.____

KNOCKING ON HEAVEN'S DOOR

Words and Music by
BOB DYLAN

Moderately slow ♩ = 69

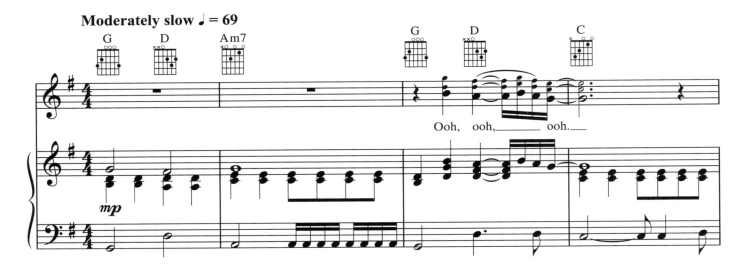

Ooh, ooh,_____ ooh._____

Ooh, ooh,_____ ooh._____

Verse:

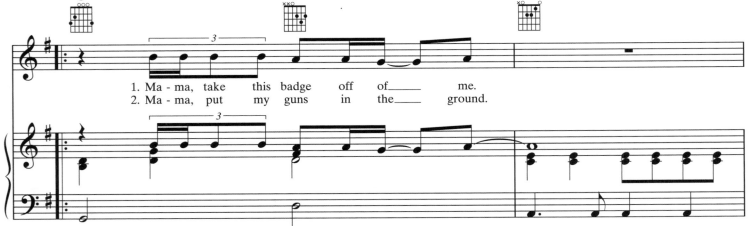

1. Ma - ma, take this badge off of_____ me.
2. Ma - ma, put my guns in the_____ ground.

LAYLA

Words and Music by
ERIC CLAPTON and JIM GORDON

Layla - 7 - 1

228

LIKE A PRAYER

Words and Music by
MADONNA CICCONE
and PAT LEONARD

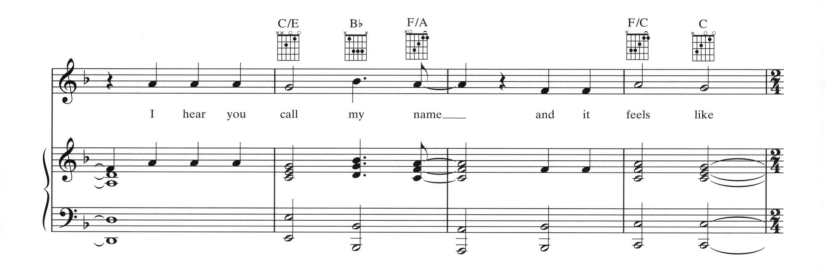

Life is a mys - ter - y, ev - 'ry - one must stand a - lone.

I hear you call my name____ and it feels like

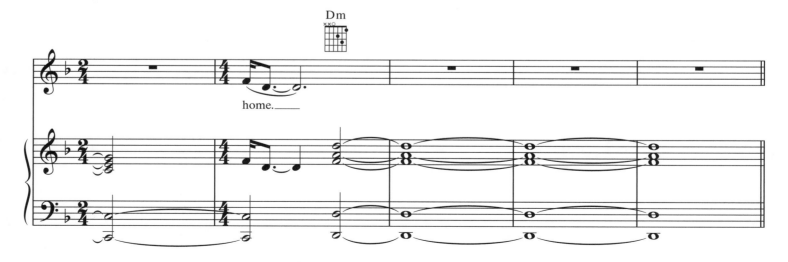

home.____

LOLA

Words and Music by
RAY DAVIES

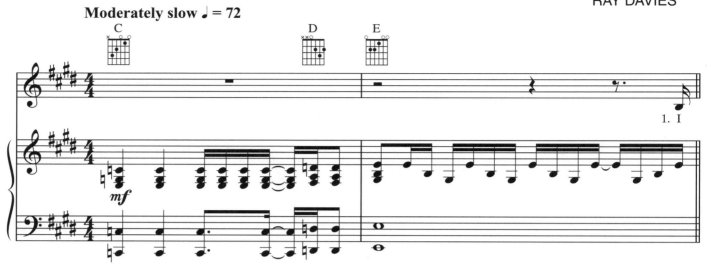

Verses 1 & 2:

met her in a club down in old So - ho_____ where you
(2.) I'm not the world's most phys - i - cal guy,_____ but when she

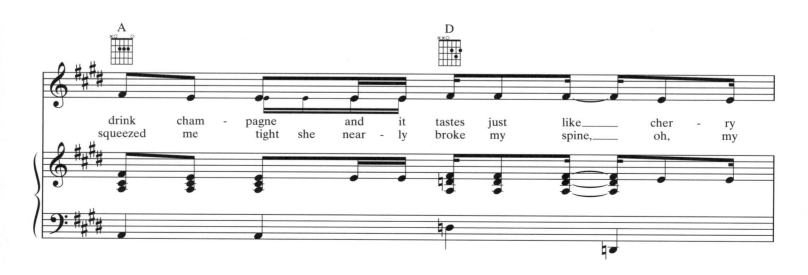

drink cham - pagne and it tastes just like_____ cher - ry
squeezed me tight she near - ly broke my spine,_____ oh, my

Lola - 6 - 1

Bridges 1 & 3:

drank cham-pagne and danced__ all night__ un-der e-lec-tric can - dle-light.__ She
I left home just a week be - fore,__ and I'd nev-er ev-er kissed a wom-an be - fore, when

picked me up___ and sat me on her knee__ and said, "Dear boy, won't you come home with me?" 3. Well,
Lo - la smiled__ and took me by the hand,__ and said, "Dear boy, I'm gon - na make you a man." 5. Well,

Verses 3 & 5:

I'm not the world's most pas - sion - ate guy,__ but when I looked in her eyes, well, I al - most fell__ for my
I'm not the world most mas - cu - line man,__ but__ I know what I am and I'm glad I'm a man and so's

Bridge 2:

LOSING MY RELIGION

Words and Music by
WILLIAM BERRY, PETER BUCK,
MICHAEL MILLS and MICHAEL STIPE

250

MAGGIE MAY

Words and Music by
ROD STEWART and MARTIN QUITTENTON

Maggie May - 4 - 1

1. Mag-gie, I wish I'd nev - er seen_ your_ face.
(2.) get on back home_____ one of these days.___
3. 4. *(etc.) Instr. repeat ad lib. and fade*

Repeat ad lib. and fade

2. I'll

Verse 2:
The morning sun, when it's in your face, really shows your age.
But that don't worry me none; in my eyes you're ev'rything.
I laughed at all of your jokes; my love you didn't need to coax.
Oh, Maggie, I couldn't have tried any more.
You led me away home, just to save you from being alone.
You stole my soul, and that's a pain I can do without.

Verse 3:
All I needed was a friend to lend a guiding hand.
But you turned into a lover, and, Mother, what a lover! You wore me out.
All you did was wreck my bed, and in the morning kick me in the head.
Oh, Maggie, I couldn't have tried any more.
You led me away home, 'cause you didn't want to be alone.
You stole my heart; I couldn't leave you if I tried.

Verse 4:
I suppose I could collect my books and get on back to school,
Or steal my Daddy's cue and make a living out of playin' pool,
Or find myself a rock 'n' roll band that needs a helpin' hand.
Oh, Maggie, I wish I'd never seen your face.
You made a first-class fool out of me, but I'm as blind as a fool can be.
You stole my heart, but I love you anyway.

THE MESSAGE

Words and Music by
SYLVIA ROBINSON, MELVIN GLOVER,
EDWARD FLETCHER and CLIFTON CHASE

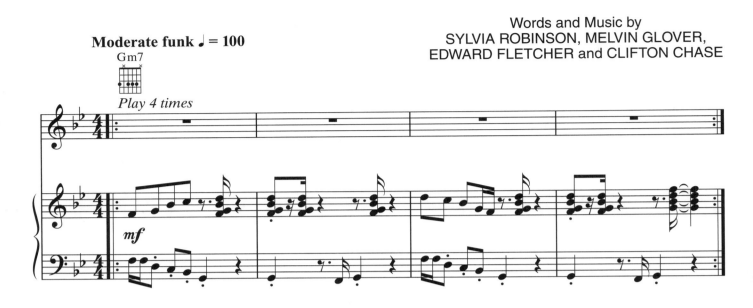

It's like a jun-gle some-times,_ it makes me won-der how I keep from go-in' un-der.

It's like a jun-gle some-times,_ it makes me won-der how I keep from go-in' un-der.

The Message - 6 - 1

Chorus:

man with the tow truck repossessed my car. Don't push__ me, 'cause__ I'm

close to___ the edge. I'm try - ing not__ to

lose my__ head. Huh-huh - huh - huh-huh. It's like a jun-gle some - times,__ it makes me won-der how I

keep from go - in' un - der.

2. Standin' on the front stoop, hangin' out the window,
3.4.5. See additional lyrics

watching all the cars go by, roaring as the breezes blow. Crazy lady, livin' in a bag,

eatin' out of garbage piles, used to be a fag-hag. Search and test a tango, skips the life and then go to

search a prince, she seems to lost her senses. Down at the peep show, watching all the creeps, so

she can tell the stories to the girls back home. She went to the city and got social security. She

Chorus:

had to get a pimp, she couldn't make it on her own. Don't push_ me, 'cause_ I'm

close to_ the edge. I'm try - ing not_ to

lose my_ head. Huh-huh - huh - huh-huh. It's like a jun-gle some - times,_ it makes me won-der how I

keep from go-in' un - der. It's like a jun-gle some-times,_ it makes me won-der how I

1.–3.

4.

keep from go - in' un - der.

3. My
4. My
5. A

keep from go - in' un - der.

It's like a jun - gle some - times,__ it makes me won - der how I keep from go - in' un - der.

Repeat and fade

It's like a jun - gle some - times,__ it makes me won - der how I keep from go - in' un - der.

Verse 3:
My brother's doin' fast on my mother's TV.
Says she watches too much, is just not healthy.
"All My Children" in the daytime, "Dallas" at night,
can't even see the game or the Sugar Ray fight.
Bill collectors, they ring my phone
and scare my wife when I'm not home.
Got a bum education, double-digit inflation,
can't take the train to the job–there's a strike
at the station. Me on King Kong, standin' on my back.
Can't stop to turn around, broke my sacroiliac.
Midrange, migraine, cancered membrane, sometimes
I think I'm going insane. I swear, I might hijack a plane.

Verse 4:
My son said, "Daddy, I don't wanna go to school, 'cause the teacher's a jerk.
He must think I'm a fool."
And all the kids smoke reefer, I think it'd be cheaper if I just got a job,
learned to be a street sweeper. I dance to the beat, shuffle my feet,
wear a shirt and tie and run with the creeps. 'Cause it's all about money,
ain't a damn thing funny. You got to have a con in this land of milk and honey.
They push that girl in front of a train, took her to a doctor,
sowed the arm on again. Stabbed that man right in his heart, gave him a
transplant before a brand-new start. I can't walk through the park, 'cause it's
crazy after the dark. Keep my hand on the gun, 'cause they got me on the run.
I feel like an outlaw, broke my last fast jaw. Hear them say you want some more,
livin' on a seesaw.

Verse 5:
A child was born, with no state of mind, blind to the ways of mankind. God is smiling on you, but he's frowning, too, 'cause only God knows
what you go through. You grow in the ghetto, living second rate, and your eyes will sing a song of deep hate. The places you play and where you stay,
looks like one great big alleyway. You'll admire all the number book takers, thugs, pimps, pushers, and the big money makers, driving big cars,
spending twenties and tens. And you wanna grow up to be just like them. Smugglers, scrambles, burglars, gamblers, pickpockets, peddlers and even
pan-handlers. You say I'm cool, I'm no fool, but then you wind up dropping out of high school. Now you're unemployed, all null 'n' void,
walkin' around like you're Pretty Boy Floyd. Turned stick-up kid, look what you done did. Got send up for a eight-year bid.
Now your man is took and you're a May-Tag, spend the next two years as an undercover fag. Being used and abused, and served like hell,
till one day you was find hung dead in a cell. It was plain to see that your life was lost. You was cold and your body swung back and forth.
But now your eyes sing the sad, sad song of how you lived so fast and died so young.

MOONDANCE

Words and Music by
VAN MORRISON

Moondance - 5 - 1

NO WOMAN, NO CRY

Words and Music by
VINCENT FORD

No Woman, No Cry - 7 - 1

270

No Woman, No Cry - 7 - 4

O-O-H CHILD

Words and Music by
STAN VINCENT

O-o-h Child - 5 - 1

PARANOID

Words and Music by
FRANK IOMMI, JOHN OSBOURNE,
WILLIAM WARD and TERENCE BUTLER

Fin-ished with__ my wom - an 'cause__ she could-n't help__ me with my mind.

I need some - one to____ show me__ the things in life____ that I can't find.

Peo - ple think__ I'm in - sane be - cause I can't see____ the things__ that make__ true

Paranoid - 5 - 1

Lyrics (bottom system): And so as___ you hear___ these words___ tell - ing___ you now___ of___

PARANOID ANDROID

Words and Music by
EDWARD O'BRIEN, PHILIP SELWAY,
JONATHAN GREENWOOD, COLIN GREENWOOD
and THOMAS YORKE

1. Please, could you stop the noise? I'm try'n' to get some rest

2. When I am King, you will be first a-gainst the wall

* Cue notes 2nd verse only.

Paranoid Android - 7 - 1

288

...end solo)

Slower ♩ = 63

Ah,_____ ah,_____

ah,_____ ah._____

Rain down, rain down,___ come on, rain down on___ me

from a great height, from a great__ height,_____ height._____

That's it, sir; you're leav-ing the crack-le of pig-skin, the dust and the scream-ing,

the yup-pies net-work-ing, ah, the pan-ic, the vom-it, the pan-ic, the vom-it.

Tempo I ♩ = **84**

God loves his chil-dren. God loves his chil-dren, yeah.

290

PERSONALITY CRISIS

Words and Music by
DAVID JOHANSEN and
JOHNNY THUNDERS

Verse 1:

You got to con - tra - dict all those times you but - ter -

To Coda ⊕ *Chorus:*

flied__ a - bout. *You was but - ter - fly'n'* 'bout a per - son - al - i - ty cri -

sis; you got it while it was hot. It's al - ways hot. You know it's

frus - tra - tion and heart - ache is what you got.__ *Ow!*

Chorus:

It's just a per-son-al-i-ty cri-sis; please don't stop, be-cause you walk a per-son-al-i-ty, talk___ ___ a per-son-al-i-ty.___

rit.

Verse 3:
Now, with all the trust and faith that Mother Nature sends,
Your mirror's gettin' jammed-up with all your friends.
That's personality; everything is starting to blend, just like it's one, one.
Personality; when your mind starts to blend.
Got so much personality, 'specially of a friend of a friend
Of a friend of a friend of a friend.
(To Coda)

RAMBLE ON

Words and Music by
JIMMY PAGE and ROBERT PLANT

Bass enters 2nd time

Verse:

1. Leaves are fall - in' all a - round,
2. 3. *See additional lyrics*

it's

time I was on my way.

Verse 2:
Got no time to for spreadin' roots,
The time has come to be gone.
And though our health we drank a thousand times,
It's time to ramble on.
(To Guitar solo:)

Verse 3:
Mine's a tale that can't be told,
My freedom I hold dear.
How years ago in days of old,
When magic filled the air,
T'was in the darkest depths of Mordor,
I met a girl so fair.
But Gollum, and the evil one,
Crept up and slipped away with her, her, her, her, her, yeah,
There ain't nothing I can do, no.
I guess I'll keep on...
(To Coda)

RAPPER'S DELIGHT

Words and Music by
BERNARD EDWARDS and NILE RODGERS

Moderate funk ♩ = 112

N.C.

Rap: 1. Now, what you hear is not a test. I'm rappin' to the beat. And
2.–9. See additional lyrics

mf

Em7

me, the groove, and my friends are gonna try to move your feet. See, I am Wonder Mike and I'd

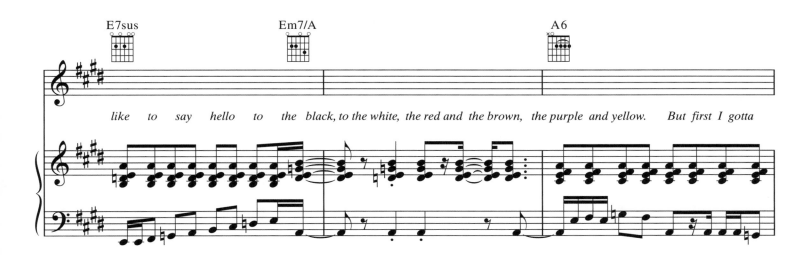

E7sus   Em7/A   A6

like to say hello to the black, to the white, the red and the brown, the purple and yellow. But first I gotta

Rapper's Delight - 3 - 1

Verse 2:
Check it out, I'm the c-a-s-an-the-o-v-a and the rest is f-l-y.
Ya see, I go by the code of the doctor of the mix
and these reasons I'll tell ya why.
Ya see, I'm six foot one and I'm tons of fun and I dress to a "T."
Ya see, I got more clothes than Muhammad Ali and I dress so viciously.
I got bodyguards, I got two big cars that definitely ain't the wack.
I got a Lincoln Continental and a sunroof Cadillac.
So after school, I take a dip in the pool, which really is on the wall.
I got a color TV so I can see the Knicks play basketball.

Verse 3:
Hear me talkin' 'bout checkbooks, credit cards,
more money than a sucker could ever spend.
But I wouldn't give a sucker or a bum from the rucker,
not a dime till I made it again.
Everybody go hotel, motel, whatcha gonna do today? (Say what?)
Ya say I'm gonna get a fly girl, gonna get some spankin',
drive off in a def o-j. Everybody go, hotel, motel, Holiday Inn.
Say if your girl starts actin' up, then you take her friend.
Master Gee, am I mellow. It's on you, so what you gonna do?

Verse 4:
Well, it's on 'n' on 'n' on on 'n' on.
The beat don't stop until the break of dawn.
I said, "M-A-S-T-E-R a G with a double E."
I said, I go by the unforgettable name
of the man they call the Master Gee.
Well, my name is known all over the world
by all the foxy ladies and the pretty girls.
I'm goin' down in history as the baddest rapper there ever could be.
Now, I'm feelin' the highs and ya feelin' the lows,
the beat starts gettin' into your toes.
Ya start poppin' your fingers and stompin' your feet,
and movin' your body while youre sittin' in your seat.
And then, damn, ya start doin' the freak.
I said, damn, right outta your seat.
Then ya throw your hands high in the air,
ya rockin' to the rhythm, shake your derriere.

Verse 5:
Ya rockin' to the beat without a care,
with the sureshot M.C.s for the affair.
Now, I'm not as tall as the rest of the gang,
but I rap to the beat just the same.
I got a little face and a pair of brown eyes.
All I'm here to do, ladies, is hypnotize.
Singin' on 'n' 'n' on 'n' on on 'n' on.
The beat don't stop until the break of dawn.
Singin' on 'n' 'n' on 'n' on on 'n' on,
like a hot buttered a-pop da pop da pop dibbie dibbie
pop da pop pop ya don't dare stop.
Come alive, y'all, gimme what ya got.
I guess by now you can take a hunch
and find that I am the baby of the bunch.
But that's okay, I still keep in stride,
'cause all I'm here to do is just wiggle your behind.

Verse 6.
Singin' on 'n' 'n' on 'n' on on 'n' on.
The beat don't stop until the break of dawn.
Singin' on 'n' 'n' on 'n' on on 'n' on.
Rock, rock, y'all, throw it on the floor.
I'm gonna freak ya here, I'm gonna freak ya there.
I'm gonna move you outta this atmosphere.
'Cause I'm one of a kind and I'll shock your mind.
I'll put t-t-tickets in your behind.
I said, 1-2-3-4, come on, girls, get on the floor.
A-come alive, y'all, a-gimme what ya got,
'cause I'm guaranteed to make you rock.
I said, 1-2-3-4, tell me, Wonder Mike, what are you waitin for?

Verse 7:
I said, a-hip hop the hippie to the hippie
the hip hip hop, a-you don't stop.
The rock it to the bang-bang boogie, say up jumped the boogie,
to the rhythm of the boogie, the beat.
Skiddlee beebop a-we rock a-scoobie doo.
And guess what, America? We love you,
'cause ya rock and ya roll with so much soul.
You could rock till you're a hundred and one years old.
I don't mean to brag, I don't mean to boast,
but we like hot butter on our breakfast toast.
Rock it up, baby bubbah, baby bubbah, to the boogie da
bang bang da boogie to the beat beat, it's so unique.
Come on, everybody, and dance to the beat.

Verse 8:
Ever went over a friend's house to eat,
and the food just ain't no good?
I mean the macaroni's soggy, the peas are mushed,
and the chicken tastes like wood.
So you try to play it off like you think you can,
by sayin' that you're full.
And then your friend says, "Momma, he's just being polite,
he ain't finished, uh-uh, that's bull."
So your heart starts pumpin' and you think of a lie,
and you say that you already ate.
And your friend says, "Man, there's plenty of food."
So you pile some more on your plate.
While the stinky food's steamin', your mind starts to dreamin'
of the moment that it's time to leave.
And then you look at your plate and your chickens slowly rottin'
into something that looks like cheese.
Oh, so you say, "That's it, I got to leave this place.
I don't care what these people think.
I'm just sittin' here makin' myself nauseous
with this ugly food that stinks."

Verse 9:
So you bust out the door while it's still closed,
still sick from the food you ate.
And then you run to the store for quick relief
from a bottle of Kaopectate.
And then you call your friend two weeks later
to see how he has been.
And he says, "I understand about the food, baby bubbah,
but we're still friends." With a hip hop the hippie to the hippie
the hip hip a hop, a-you don't stop the rockin'
to the bang bang boogie.
Say up jump the boogie to the rhythm of the boogie, the beat.

REDEMPTION SONG

Words and Music by
BOB MARLEY

RUNNING ON EMPTY

Words and Music by
JACKSON BROWNE

Running on Empty - 8 - 1

Ev-'ry-one I know,___ ev-'ry-where I go,___

SAIL AWAY

Slowly ♩ = 63

Words and Music by
RANDY NEWMAN

Sail Away - 5 - 1

With a beat

Ain't no lion__ or ti - ger,__ ain't no mam - ba snake,__

just the sweet__ wa - ter - mel - on and the buck - wheat cake.

Ev - 'ry - bod - y is as hap - py as a man can be;___

climb a - board, lit - tle wog, sail a - way with me. Sail a -

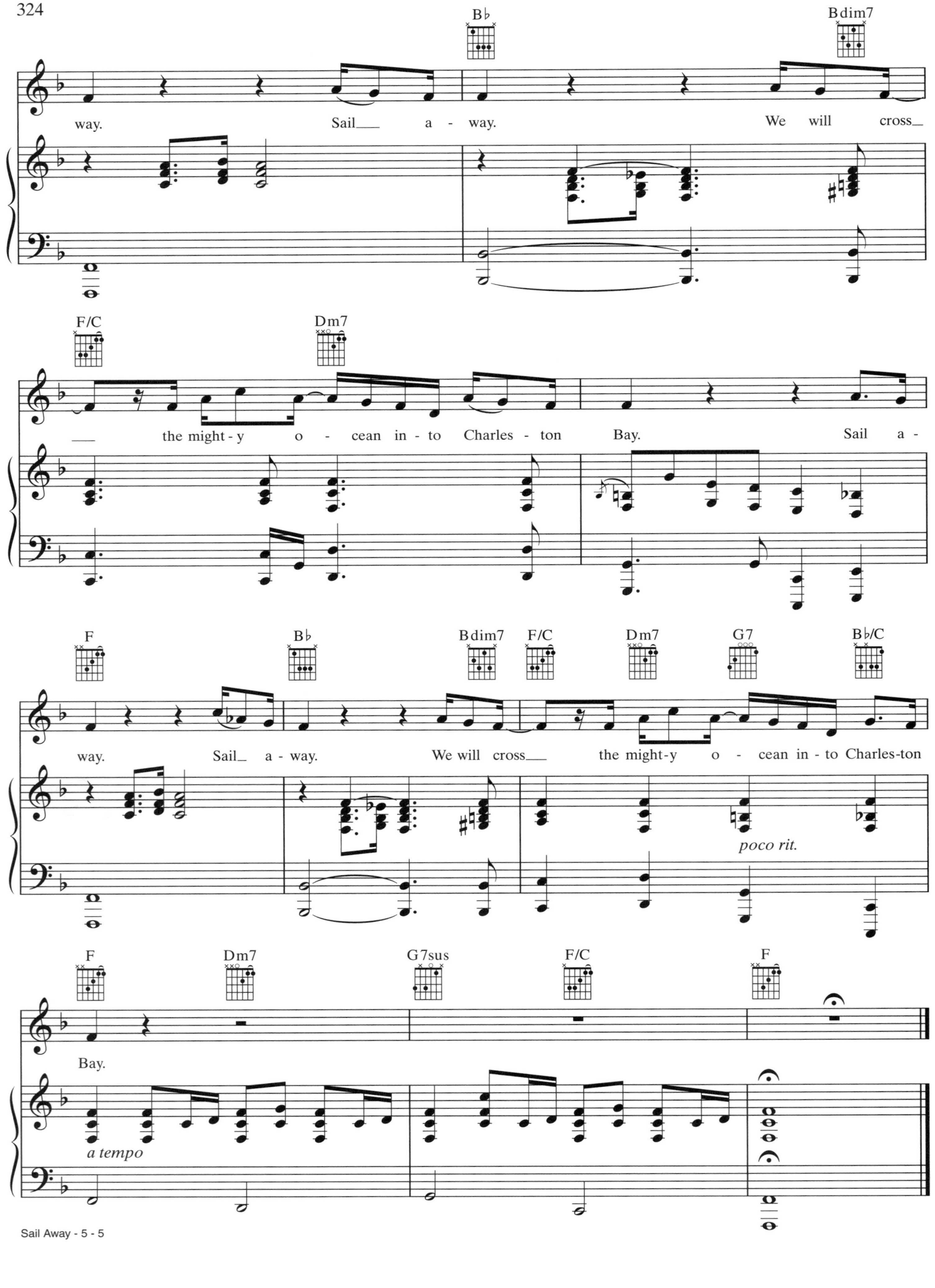

B♭
Bdim7
way. Sail__ a - way. We will cross__
F/C
Dm7
__ the might-y o - cean in - to Charles - ton Bay. Sail a -
F
B♭
Bdim7
F/C
Dm7
G7
B♭/C
way. Sail_ a - way. We will cross__ the might-y o - cean in - to Charles-ton
poco rit.
F
Dm7
G7sus
F/C
F
Bay.
a tempo

THUNDER ROAD

Words and Music by
BRUCE SPRINGSTEEN

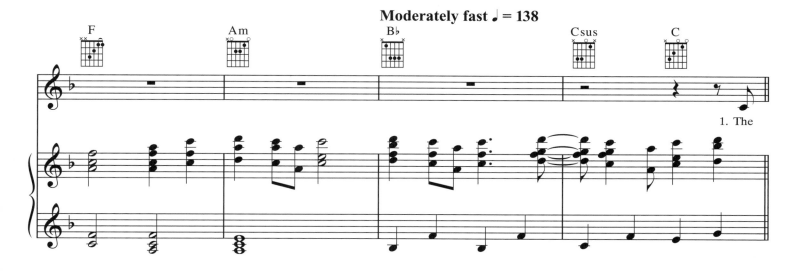

Thunder Road - 9 - 1

night's bust-ing o-pen, these_ two lanes will take us an - y - where. We got

one last chance_ to make it real,_ to trade_ in these wings_ on some wheels.

Climb in_ back, heav - en's_ wait-ing down on_ the tracks._

Chorus:

Oh,_ come take_ my hand,_ rid-ing out to-night to_ case the prom-ised land.

Thunder Road - 9 - 5

STAIRWAY TO HEAVEN

Words and Music by
JIMMY PAGE and ROBERT PLANT

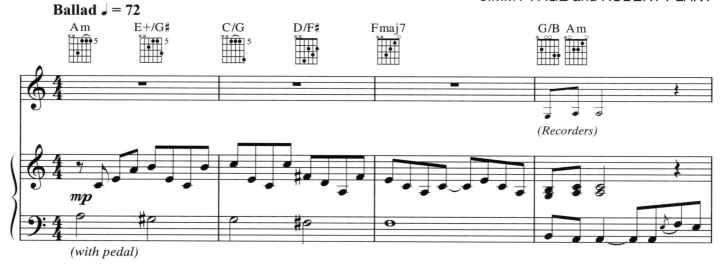

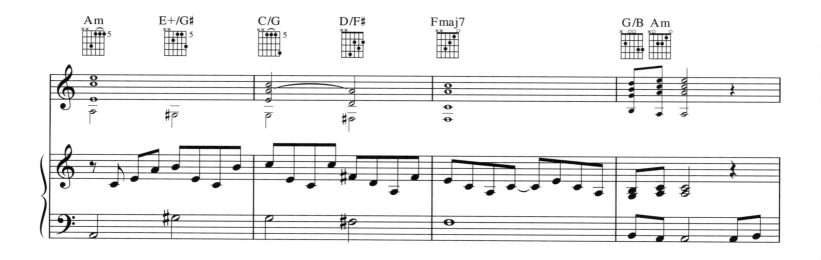

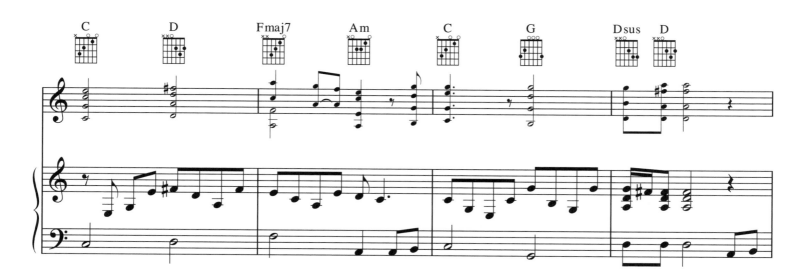

Repeat as desired for solo

solo continues

And as we wind on down the road, our shad-ow's tall-er than our soul.

STAYIN' ALIVE

Words and Music by
BARRY GIBB, MAURICE GIBB
and ROBIN GIBB

Moderate disco beat ♩ = 108

1. Well, you can tell

Verses 1, 3:

___ (1. 3.) by the way I use___ my walk,___ I'm a wom - an's man; no time to talk.___

Verse 2:

___ (2.) get___ low___ and I ___ get high,___ and if I can't get ei - ther, I real - ly try. Got the

Stayin' Alive - 6 - 1

Mu - sic loud__ and wom - en warm,_ I've been kicked a - round_ since I___ was born. And now it's

wings of heav - en on___ my shoes._ I'm a danc - in' man and I just__ can't lose.__ You know it's

(1. 2. 3.) all right,__ it's o - kay,__ and you may look__ the oth - er way,__ but

we can try___ to un - der - stand__ the New York Times'_ ef - fect__ on man.__

346

Chorus:

Life go - in' no - where._____

Some - bod - y help___ me, yeah.___

I'm stay - in' a - live._

D.S. 𝄋 *al Coda*

3. Well, you can tell_

⊕ *Coda*

Life go - in' no - where._____

Repeat ad lib. and fade

SWEET CHILD O' MINE

Words and Music by
STEVEN ADLER, SAUL HUDSON,
DUFF MCKAGAN, W. AXL ROSE
and IZZY STRADLIN

Moderate rock ♩ = 126

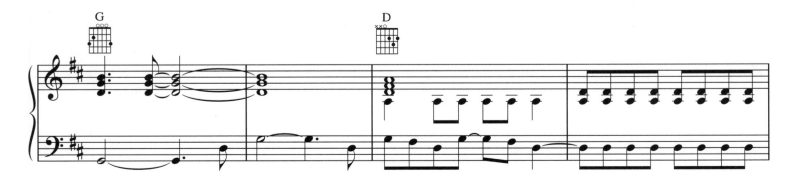

*Original recording in D♭, all guitars tuned down 1/2 step.

Sweet Child O' Mine - 8 - 1

Verse:

1. She's got a smile_ that it seems to me_ re-minds_ me of child - hood
2. She's got eyes_ of the blu-est skies,_ as if they thought of rain._

mem-o-ries_ where ev - 'ry-thing_ was as fresh_ as the bright_ blue sky._
_____ I hate to look in - to those eyes___ and

Whoa, oh,___ oh, oh,_____ sweet love o' mine.___
oh, oh, oh,_____ sweet love o' mine.___

Chorus:

Woah, oh,__ oh, oh,_____ sweet child of mine._____ Ooh,_____

oh, oh,__ oh,_____ oh,_____ sweet love of mine.__

Whoa, oh,__ oh, oh,_____ sweet child_ of mine._____ Ooh,__ yeah.__

THANK YOU
(Falettinme Be Mice Elf Agin)

Words and Music by
SYLVESTER STEWART

Moderate funk ♩ = 108

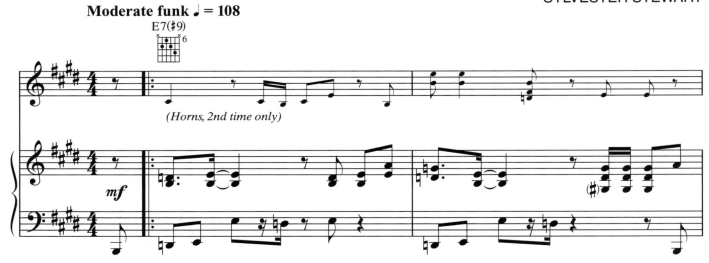

(Horns, 2nd time only)

Verses 1, 2, & 3:
E7(♯9)

1. Look - in' at the dev - il,
2. Stiff all in the col - lar;
3. Dance___ to the mu - sic

Thank You (Falettinme Be Mice Elf Agin) - 6 - 1

grin - nin' at his gun.___
fluff - y in the face.___
all___ night___ long.___

Fin - gers start shak - in';
Chit - chat chat - ter try - in';
Ev - 'ry - day peo - ple

I be - gin to run.___
stuff - y in the place.___
sing a sim - ple song.___

Bul - lets start chas - in';
Thank you for the par - ty,
Ma - ma's so hap - py,

but

gin.___

Thank you fa - let-tin-me be mice elf___ a - gin.___

1.2.

N.C.

3.

362

Verse 4:

4. Flam - in' eyes___ of peo-ple's fears___ burn - in' in - to you.___

Man - y men___ are miss - in' much,___ hat - in' what they do.___

Youth and truth___ are mak - in' love;___ dig it for a start - er.

Dy - in' young___ is hard to take;___ sell - in' out is hard - er.

Chorus:

Thank you fa - let - tin - me be mice elf____ a -

gin.____ I_____ want to

thank you fa - let - tin - me be mice elf____ a -

Repeat ad lib. and fade

gin.____ I_____ want to

WALK ON THE WILD SIDE

Words and Music by
LOU REED

Moderately ♩ = 96

1. Hol - ly came from Mi - am - i, F - L - A.,
2.–5. See additional lyrics

hitch - hiked her way a - cross the U. S. A.

Plucked her eye - brows on the way, shaved her legs and then *he was a she. She says,*

Verse 2:
Candy came from out on the Island.
In the backroom, she was everybodys darling.
But she never lost her head,
Even when she was givin' head.
She says, "Hey, babe, take a walk on the wild side."
Said, "Hey, babe, take a walk on the wild side."

Verse 3:
Little Joe never once gave it away.
Everybody had to pay and pay.
A hustle here and a hustle there.
New York City is the place where they said,
"Hey, babe, take a walk on the wild side."
I said, "Hey, Joe, take a walk on the wild side."

Verse 4:
Sugar Plum Fairy came and hit the streets,
Lookin' for soul food and a place to eat.
Went to the Apollo,
You should have seen him go-go-go.
They said, "Hey, sugar, take a walk on the wild side."
I said, "Hey, babe, take a walk on the wild side."
All right, huh.

Verse 5:
Jackie is just speeding away.
Thought she was James Dean for a day.
Then I guess she had to crash,
Valium would have helped that dash.
She said, "Hey, babe, take a walk on the wild side."
I said, "Hey, honey, take a walk on the wild side."

WHAT'S GOING ON

Words and Music by
MARVIN GAYE, AL CLEVELAND
and RENALDO BENSON

Moderate R&B ♩ = 96

there's far too man-y of you dy___ ing. You___ know__ we've
for on-ly love can con-quer___ hate.___ You___ know__ we've
sim-ply 'cause our hair is___ long.___ You___ know__ we've

got to find__ a way__ to bring some lov-in' here to-day,___
got to find__ a way__ to bring some
got to find__ a way__ to bring some un-der-

yeah.___
lov-in' here to-day,___ oh.
stand-ing here to-day,___ oh.___

Chorus:

Pick-et lines__ and pick-et signs,__ don't pun-ish me with__ bru-
{ (Sis - ter, sis - ter, sis - ter,
(Broth-er, broth-er, broth-er,

Repeat ad lib. and fade

WILD HORSES

Words and Music by
MICK JAGGER and KEITH RICHARDS

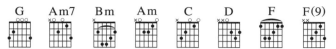

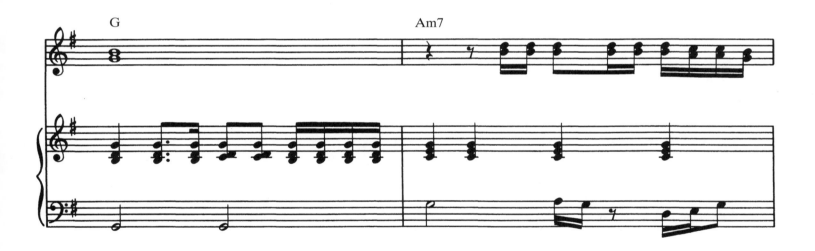

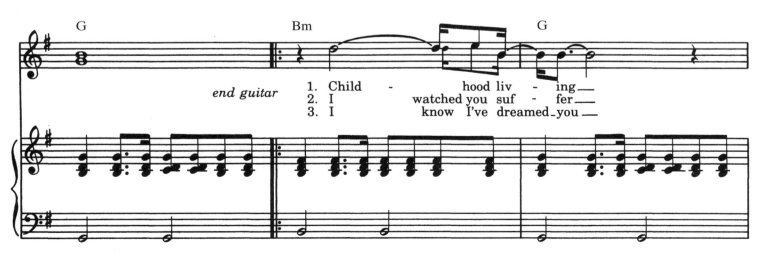

*Lead guitar:

end guitar

1. Child - hood liv - ing —
2. I watched you suf - fer —
3. I know I've dreamed you —

* *8va if played by Guitar.*

Wild Horses - 5 - 1

* 8va if played by Guitar.

we'll ride them some-day.

*Guitar:

D. S. 𝄋 al Coda

end guitar

Coda

we'll ride them___ some - day.

* 8va if played by Guitar.

WISH YOU WERE HERE

Words and Music by
ROGER WATERS and DAVID GILMOUR

Slow rock feel (♩ = 63)

(2nd time - Acoustic Guitar solo ad lib.)

(end solo)

Verse 1:

So,_____ so you think you can tell_____ heav-en from hell,

fears._____   Wish you_____ were here._____

Ending:

(2nd time - Dobro doubled by scat vocal cont.)

Repeat and fade

(1st time - Dobro doubled by scat vocal)

383